M000035480

SELECT STUDIES

IN

RESTORATION HISTORY

1700-PRESENT DAY

ANDREW D. ERWIN

Charleston, AR

COBB PUBLISHING

2017

Gospel Gleaner Publications

PO Box 456

Fayetteville, TN 37334

www.gospelgleaner.com

andyerwin@gospelgleaner.com

© 2017 by Andrew D. Erwin

Published in the United States of America by Gospel Gleaner Publications

ISBN: 978-1947622012

Published by:

Cobb Publishing
704 E. Main St.
Charleston, AR 72933

(479) 747-8372
www.CobbPublishing.com
CobbPublishing@gmail.com

Preface

Select Studies in Restoration History is the result of the author's teaching classes on the subject of Restoration History over the course of several years. The book is divided into thirteen chapters, which will enable churches and schools to use these lessons in quarterly class settings.

The reader will find that the historical study of churches of Christ in America is brought into the present day. This study provides a *"Reader's Digest"* approach to the Restoration Movement.

A lot of ground is covered in a relatively small book. Thus, the reader will observe that much more could and should be said about many of the people and events we shall consider. For further study, we have listed various sources at the conclusion of the book.

The reader will also observe that references are given to sources within the body of the text rather than in footnotes or endnotes. Statistics shown throughout the book come from a variety of sources. Older statistics are derived from US censuses and brotherhood periodicals. More recent statistics are derived from directories published by the *Firm Foundation* and *Twenty-First Century Christian*.

Dedication

I would like to offer a heartfelt word of thanks to the staff writers of the *Gospel Gleaner*. It has been my privilege to work with these good men in spreading God's word through the written page. For your labor of love in the Kingdom, this volume is affectionately dedicated.

Andy Erwin

Table of Contents

Chapter One

The Beginnings of the Restoration Movement

1700-1810

"Scotch-Irish" Influences on the Restoration Movement

In the early 18th Century a prevailing insistence for the absolute authority of the Scriptures was evident in Scotland, parts of Ireland, and England. A number of prominent and scholarly religious reformers wanted the Bible to be accepted as the sole rule for their faith and practice, and pleaded for the independence and autonomy of the local congregations.

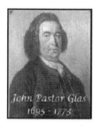

John Glas (1695–1773) was a Presbyterian minister who called for a separation of church and state. We can appreciate him for seeing the need for the church to be recognized separately from the state, calling for congregational autonomy, and elders to oversee the local church.

Robert Sandeman (1718–1771) was a son-in-law of John Glas. He was an effective evangelist in Scotland and in the New England Colonies where he died.

In 1757 he published *Letters on Theron and Aspasio*, in which he stood strongly against the doctrine of "imputed righteousness" as taught by Calvinism. In 1760, his *Letters* was published in New England, which led to a 1763 invitation to Danbury, Connecticut in America to advise on church formation.

Sandeman helped to organize a few small congregations in America. These congregations came to be recognized for their weekly observance of the Lord's Supper, weekly contribution, congregational autonomy, and plurality of elders. They were also known for their rejection of creeds and confessions of faith.

 **Robert** (1764-1842) and **James** (1768-1851) **Haldane** must also be considered in our study. In 1797 **Robert Haldane** sold his castle, left the Church of Scotland because of its cold formalism, and joined his brother and some others in the formation of the "Society for the Propagation of the Gospel at Home," in building chapels or "tabernacles" for congregations, in supporting missionaries, and in maintaining institutions for the education of young men to carry on the work of evangelization. Within nine years they had organized eighty-five churches, including one in Rich Hill, Ireland, where Thomas Campbell and his family would later live and preach for the Presbyterian Church.

James Alexander Haldane began preaching for a large Independent congregation in Edinburgh in 1799. This was the first congregational church known by that name in Scotland. He ministered to this congregation for more than fifty years.

 **Thomas Campbell** was born February 1, 1763 in County Down, Ireland. He was born to parents who were devout and God-fearing people. His father was at first a Catholic and then became a member of the Church of England.

Thomas was educated at the University of Glasgow (1783-1786). After graduating from Glasgow, he entered the theological seminary of the Anti-Burgher Seceder Presbyterian Church, conducted by Archibald Bruce at Whitburn (midway between Edinburgh and Glasgow). Here, Thomas attended 8-week sessions for 5 years (1787-1791). His father wanted him to enter the ministry of the Church of England, so Thomas' decision to join the Church of the Succession greatly displeased him.

The Seceder Movement began with the General Assembly's decision to take away from the local church the right of selecting preachers. Ebenezer Erskine was instrumental in protesting this decision. Later the Seceders would divide over the issue of oaths. The burgesses (magistrates) of the towns required oaths of the people, requiring them to support the religion of that district. Those who considered the oath unlawful were known as "**Anti-burghers**." The final division to affect Thomas Campbell was whether to be a "**New Light**" or "**Old Light**" on the question of whether or not the Solemn League and Covenant (a treaty between England and Scotland which was meant to preserve the reformed religion of Scotland) should be made a term of communion. Thomas Campbell was therefore an Old Light Anti-Burgher in the Seceder Presbyterian Church.

During the years 1798-1807, Thomas Campbell served as the Pastor of this branch of the Presbyterian Church in Rich Hill, Ireland. It was here, especially, that he and his family were intrigued by the teachings of John Glas. Often, the Campbell family visited the services of the Independent "Glasite" church in Rich Hill where James Haldane preached.

In 1807, for health and family reasons, Thomas Campbell decided to move to America. He departed from Londonderry, Ireland on the ship *Brutus*, on April 1, 1807. His family was to arrive later, after he had made all the necessary arrangements. The voyage lasted thirty-five days. Thomas Campbell was forty-five years old at the time.

Alexander Campbell (1788-1866), born September 12, 1788 in County Antrip, Ireland, was but a young man of nineteen years when his father left for America. He had been well-trained by his father and two uncles (Enos and

Archibald) to read extensively in literature, philosophy, and religion. While he was at home as a boy, he had memorized Proverbs, Ecclesiastes, and many of the Psalms. He was also raised to witness his father's efforts to unite a divided Presbyterian cause.

While at Rich Hill his father had begun an academy which, upon his departure for America, he left in the hands of young Alexander. It was while he was awaiting his own voyage to America that Alexander received perhaps his greatest opportunity.

The family departed for America on October 1, 1808, on the ship *Hibernia*. On the evening of October 7, it struck a rock and began to fill with water. All of the passengers on the ship were saved, but another boat could not be secured so late in the sailing season.

Alexander took this opportunity to enroll in the University of Glasgow for one year, where he studied Greek, French, logic, and philosophy. Through the influence of Grenville Ewing, Alexander was introduced to the teachings of James and Robert Haldane. While in Scotland, he also became familiar with the views of John Glas and Robert Sandeman.

While in Glasgow, Alexander severed himself from the Seceder Church and came to think of himself in more "independent" terms. He later wrote about this period of his life, saying:

> "My faith in creeds and confessions of human device was considerably shaken while in Scotland, and I commenced my career in this country under the conviction that nothing that was not as old as the New Testament should be made an article of faith…or a term of communion against Christians."

On July 31, 1809, Alexander and his family set sail for America on the *Latonia*, arriving in New York on September 29.

5

Religion and the Restoration Movement in Colonial America

From 1629-1640, 20,000 Puritans (or "Congregationalists" – a Calvinistic reform movement from within the Church of England) arrived from England to establish a "holy commonwealth" in the New World.

During the 18th Century a great Scotch-Irish migration brought many Presbyterians (Church of Scotland) to the colonies. By 1775 they were scattered throughout all the colonies and had become the second largest denomination.

In 1784 the Anglican churches in America changed their name to the Episcopal Church. Also, in 1784 at the "Christmas Conference" in Baltimore, John Wesley's "Methodist Societies" were organized into a separate church from the Church of England, taking the name Methodist Episcopal Church. It was agreed that:

> "During the Life of the Rev. Mr. Wesley, we acknowledge ourselves his in the Gospel, ready in matters belonging to Church-Government, to obey his Commands."

Wesley viewed church government as being strictly Episcopal. The church hierarchy, not the people, would choose who would serve in the church. He once wrote:

> "As long as I live the people shall have no share in choosing either stewards or leaders among the Methodists...We are no republicans and never intend to be." (Compare this statement with Acts 6:3).

The Europeans brought their religion to the New World, often hoping to escape the state-church system in Europe. However, many simply established their own form of a state-funded religious system in the colonies. By the time of the Revolution the five largest denominations were: Puritans, or Congregationalists (658 churches); Presbyterians (543); Baptists (498); Anglicans (480); and Quakers (295). Catholics (50) and Methodists (37) would become major religious powers during the 19th Century. Today the United States has over 6,000 denominations, but only one church was ever built by Christ (Matthew 16:18) or authorized by God.

The Great Awakenings

During the 1730's and 1740's the **First Great Awakening** spawned a renewal in religious interest in the colonies. The Awakening was begun by Dutch Reformists in New Jersey in 1726 and spread into the Presbyterian, Baptist, and Methodist camps. The most notable preachers of this revival were the Calvinist Jonathan Edwards and the Anglican George Whitfield.

The Great Awakening also led to many colleges being established, including Princeton. In the years following the Revolutionary War, the country was demoralized, with less than ten percent of the population claiming any religious affiliation.

A **Second Great Awakening** soon began on the Atlantic seaboard and spread as far as Kentucky, culminating with the great **Cane Ridge Revival** of 1801.

Restoration Advocated in Carolina and Virginia

James O'Kelly (1735-1826) and **Rice Haggard** (1796-1819) were Methodists who came to oppose the Methodist form of church government, and specifically Francis Asbury as the Superintendent (later *Bishop*) for the Methodist Church in America.

O'Kelly argued for the right to appeal Asbury's preaching appointments, but when that was rejected on December 25, 1792, O'Kelly walked out of the Methodist conference with about 1/2 of those in attendance.

On December 25, 1793, those who had separated from the Methodists and the Methodist Episcopal Church, because of their desire to reform Methodism, formed the "Republican Methodist Church."

On August 4, 1794 at Old Lebanon in Surry County, Virginia, James O'Kelly, Rice Haggard, and others met to devise a plan of church government.

In this meeting, "Five Cardinal Principles of the Christian Church" were devised:

1) The Lord Jesus is the only head of the church.
2) They were to be called "Christian" to the exclusion of all party and sectarian names.
3) The Bible was to be their only creed, and a sufficient rule of faith and practice.
4) Christian character was the only test of church fellowship and membership.
5) The right to private judgment and the liberty of conscience was the privilege and duty of all men.

By 1801 the "Republican Methodists" changed their name to the "Christian Church" in order to be identified with the disciples of Acts 11:26. By 1809, it was estimated that the group had grown from 6,000 in 1794 to 20,000. James O'Kelly believed in partaking of the Lord's Supper on the first day of the week, that the collection was to be a free-will offering, singing, preaching, praying, and admonishing the saints. However he did not believe baptism was necessary, but that sprinkling or pouring would suffice. He was never immersed.

Restoration Advocated in New England

 While O'Kelly was attempting to restore church government, two Baptist preachers: **Elias Smith** (1769-1846) and **Abner Jones** (1772-1841) were determined to restore the church's doctrine. Elias Smith and Abner Jones  were concerned with the Calvinism they saw corrupting the Baptist Church.

Smith and Jones could never reconcile the doctrine of Calvinism with the practice of extending and invitation for any man who would accept Christ. Upon these shared principles, Smith and Jones determined to work together to restore the ancient order of the New Testament church.

It would not be long until the New England and O'Kelly groups knew of each other. Meetings were held in 1809 and 1810 to discuss unity. However, James O'Kelly refused to unite because he did not agree with Smith and Jones on the mode of baptism. The groups merged regardless of O'Kelly, and he spent the remainder of his years in relative obscurity.

O'Kelly was not be the only leader this fledgling movement would lose. In October of 1817, Elias Smith announced his conversion to universalism. His announcement did indeed stagger the cause of restoration in New England, but not permanently.

Under the leadership of men like **Daniel Hix** and Abner Jones, the movement kept growing. Hix became a leader in the movement when he led his entire congregation, one of the largest Baptist churches in Boston, to reject denominationalism and its creed and accept the Bible as its sole rule of faith and practice.

However, a growing impulse of emotionalism and unhealthy obsession with numerical growth eventually sealed the fate of this movement. Many of these congregations were swept away by the teaching of William Miller in the 1840's and what remained later merged with the Congregational Church. Since that time, the Congregational Christian Church has merged with some other denominations and are known by the name "the United Church of Christ."

Timeline of Events

➢ **1792-1794** – James O'Kelly leaves the Methodist Church on the principle of church government and along with others forms the Republican Methodist Church. Later they reject this name and call themselves simply "Christians."

➢ **1801** – The Cane Ridge Revival has between 20,000-30,000 people attending its services.

➢ **1802** – Elias Smith rejects Calvinism and begins leading a restoration movement in New England along with Abner Jones.

➢ **1804** – Having left the Presbyterian Church (1803) because of its Calvinistic doctrines, Barton W. Stone and others began the Springfield Presbytery. They later dissolve it and take the sacred name "Christians" as their only title. Stone's influence would especially permeate through Kentucky, Tennessee, Ohio, Indiana, and Illinois.

➢ **1808** – Elias Smith began printing the *Herald of Gospel Liberty.* This paper would later be called the *Christian Herald* (1818) and the *Christian Journal* (1835).

➢ **1809** – Thomas Campbell leaves the Seceder Presbyterian Church because of sectarianism, becomes part of the Christian Association of Washington and writes the *Declaration and Address.* Alexander and the family arrived later that year.

➢ **1810** - The New England Christians merge with those of the O'Kelly group. O'Kelly does not join them.

Chapter Two

The Restoration Movement in America Continues

1811-1820

Early Work of Barton W. Stone

Barton W. Stone (1772-1844) was born in Port Tobacco, Maryland. The sudden and untimely death of his father left him with some means of an inheritance. He used this money to attend David Caldwell's school, Guilford Academy, near Greensboro, North Carolina. He entered school believing he wanted to become a lawyer or possibly a statesman.

While a student (1790-1793), Stone heard the Calvinistic message of the well-known Presbyterian evangelist James McGready and was turned sour on religion. He would later say of this message, "He left me with not one encouraging word." However, while at Guilford, Stone also heard messages from another Presbyterian preacher, William Hodge, this time on the theme of the love of God. Hodge "converted" Stone in 1791 (Stone would later be baptized along with the Cane Ridge congregation in 1804).

In 1794, Stone moved to Washington, Georgia, and taught school for a Methodist minister named Hope Hull. Hull knew and voted with James O'Kelly, but did not join him in leaving the Methodists.

Stone returned to North Carolina in 1796 and received his license to preach. He received his Presbyterian Preacher license at the session of the Orange Presbytery on April 6.

Stone then turned his attention to the west, specifically Tennessee and Kentucky. Passing through a little community of 300, Stone commented that is was "a poor little village scarcely worth the notice." That community was Nashville!

Stone arrived in Kentucky in 1796 and settled near Lexington. He was ordained by the Transylvania Presbytery (formed in 1786), and became the preacher at Cane Ridge and Concord, Kentucky. At his ordination, when asked if he would take his oath of allegiance to the Westminster Confession of Faith, Stone said, "As far as it is consistent with the word of God."

As a Presbyterian, Stone remained constantly troubled by the doctrine of Total Hereditary Depravity. He would later recall how preaching the doctrine of depravity and human helplessness, and then trying to persuade the helpless to repent, chilled his spirit at the contradiction.

To combat spiritual apathy, Stone decided to conduct a revival at Cane Ridge in August of 1801. It is estimated that between 20,000 and 30,000 people attended. Preachers from different denominations spoke at different places and times at this revival. Because salvation by faith and repentance was preached, charges were brought against Stone and four others before the Synod of Kentucky on September 6-13, 1803. Before the Synod could conduct its trial, these five men announced that they were renouncing the authority of the Synod.

As a result, the Springfield Presbytery was formed. In the *Apology of the Springfield Presbytery* you will find expressed the total abandonment of all authoritative creeds but the Bible. The Springfield Presbytery, however, lasted only nine months as Stone and the others determined it was no more scriptural than the Synod they had just renounced.

Their decision prompted the *Last Will and Testament of the Springfield Presbytery.* One other interesting note is that in 1804, while a visitor at Cane Ridge, Rice Haggard was able again to propose to a group advocating a return to the primitive church, that the sacred name "Christian" be used rather than any manmade name.

Within a year some fifteen "Christian" congregations were established in Kentucky (8) and Ohio (7). Stone began signing his name as: "Barton W. Stone, E.C.C." that is, "Elder in the Church of Christ."

Just as we find in the Book of Acts, however, when the Lord's people begin thriving and growing, Satan attempts to destroy them. In 1805 we find the "Shaker" movement invading the church.

The Shakers had several strange beliefs. This group was founded by Anna Lee on the presumption that she had received a "divine revelation." They insisted that she was now the Christ with power to save and possessed new revelations superior to the Bible. Moreover, the Shakers maintained that Christ had already returned a second time and that the resurrection and judgment were then underway. They taught that marriage was forbidden. And that the Shakers in this life would never die.

Surprisingly, two of the men who left the Presbyterians with Stone, Richard McNemar and John Dunlavy, were swept away in this movement. While their loss was very serious and grievous at the time, it may have proven to be a blessing as their fanatical tendencies would have likely only caused greater problems for the church later.

Two other signers of the "Last Will and Testament," Robert Marshall and John Thompson, later revealed that they still held orthodox Presbyterian views on the subjects of baptism and the atonement and returned to the Presbyterian Church. Stone would later comment, "Of all five of us that left the Presbyterians, I only was left, and they sought my life."

One bright spot out of this was the steadfastness of **David Purviance** (1766-1847). A Kentucky statesman from the Cane Ridge area who opposed slavery, Purviance was defeated in his bid for

another term as a state delegate and the opportunity to help frame the state constitution because of his strong anti-slavery convictions.

For a while, Purviance withdrew from politics and devoted his life to preaching. He believed he could not preach the gospel and remain in politics. In 1803, he seceded from the Presbyterian Church, and shortly after this helped to establish a church which worked and worshiped according to the New Testament pattern.

He helped to perfect the work of the old Cane Ridge Church. Purviance became an elder there and was ordained by it to preach. It is claimed that he was the first

preacher that publicly repudiated infant baptism, and he insisted that the immersion in water of a believing penitent is the only baptism taught in the New Testament. Purviance was one of the drafters and witnesses of the *Last Will and Testament of the Springfield Presbytery*.

In 1807 he moved to Ohio. He had not been there long until he was elected to the Ohio Legislature. He met with Barton W. Stone for the last time at New Paris, Ohio, in 1843. When they met in the church house, they embraced each other, and the whole congregation was moved to tears as these two heroes of the simple truth of the gospel fervently engaged in this act. It has been said that Stone and Purviance did more than any other two men in establishing the cause of primitive Christianity in Kentucky and Ohio.

Other Key Contributors

John Mulkey (1773-1844) is another man worthy of mention at this time. Mulkey was born in South Carolina, January 14, 1773 and began preaching in East Tennessee when he was 20 years old. After moving to Ken-

tucky, Mulkey decided to leave the Baptist Church, its creed, and the doctrine of unconditional election. He and his brother, Philip, would do a great work in restoring the ancient order in that area of Kentucky. Like the Cane Ridge Meetinghouse, the "Mulkey" Meetinghouse still stands today.

John Wright was another denominational preacher that came to believe in faith by the Bible alone. He became a considerable influence for restoring the ancient church in Indiana.

With men like David Purviance, John Mulkey, and John Wright to help in the cause, the church continued to grow, numbering twenty-four congregations in four states (Kentucky, Ohio, Indiana, and Tennessee) by 1807.

The Scotsman **Walter Scott** (1796-1861) came to America in 1818. He was educated at the University of Edinburgh, and he soon found an opportunity to teach Latin in an academy at Jamaica, Long Island. In the spring of 1819 he and a friend decided to see what opportunities awaited them along the Ohio River. They walked the distance from New York City to Pittsburgh, arriving in the city on May 7, 1819.

Scott began teaching at a school operated by George Forrester. Forrester was also a preacher for a small church associated with the Haldanes. Through the teaching of Forrester, Scott accepted the principle of restoring Christianity and was immersed. After Forrester's untimely death (by drowning in the Alleghany River while bathing), Scott was left to operate the school and preach for the small congregation. Also during this time, Scott began to learn that baptism was for the remission of sins (see Acts 2:38).

Early Work of the Campbell Family

Thomas Campbell arrived in America at Philadelphia on May 13, 1807. The Synod of North America was in session at Philadelphia when he arrived there. He was cordially received by the synod and was commended to preach in Washington County, Pennsylvania.

However, the spirit of sectarianism was very bitter at that time in that region. Even different branches of the Presbyterian faith refused to have fellowship with each other.

Thomas Campbell deplored such a state of affairs and sought to bring about peace between the discordant branches of the Presbyterian faith. He encouraged members of different churches to come together and eat the Lord's Supper with the members of his church (many of them went without a preacher or even church services for weeks at a time).

Campbell's attitude toward unity displeased the Presbyterian Church, and he was brought before the Chartiers Presbytery for a formal rebuke in May, 1808. Campbell plead for unity and liberality before them. However, by September, this presbytery made it clear that Campbell was no longer welcome in their midst. On September 13, 1808, Campbell formally made his break with Secederism.

He continued to preach, but was excluded from the church houses. He preached in groves and private houses. He always pleaded openly and boldly for Christian liberty and union upon the principles taught in the Bible.

People thronged to hear him. They admired him and wanted to know why he was not being permitted to preach as before.

He soon found many intelligent and pious people who were dissatisfied with religious parties and the intolerance of sectarianism which prevailed at that time.

A special meeting was called at the house of Abraham Altars, and at this meeting he declared his conviction that the word of God as revealed in the Bible was all-sufficient as a basis of union and cooperation for Christians. This condemned all creeds. He then stoutly urged all to abandon everything in religion for which there could not be produced a "Thus saith the Lord." He announced the famous statement: "Where the Scriptures speak, we speak; and where the Scriptures are silent, we are silent." This has become the slogan for all who have given up creeds and have taken the Bible alone as their rule of faith and worship in the service of God.

During this meeting a Scottish bookseller named Andrew Munro said, "Mr. Campbell, if we adopt that as a basis, then there is the end of infant baptism." Campbell answered, saying, "Of course, if infant baptism be not found in the scriptures, we can have nothing to do with it." This answer brought a very emotional reply from another attendee, Thomas Acheson. Acheson arose and cried out, "I hope I may never see the day when my heart will renounce that blessed saying of the Scripture, 'Suffer little children to come unto me and forbid them not, for of such is the kingdom of heaven.'" To which James Foster replied, "Mr. Acheson, I would remark that in the portion of Scripture you have quoted, there is no reference whatever to infant baptism."

The Christian Association of Washington and the *Declaration and Address*

On August 17, 1809, "The Christian Association of Washington" was formed. On September 8, 1809, Thomas Campbell issued his memorable *Declaration and Address*. This document came about at the insistence of a Mr. Welch. Welch fixed a room for Campbell at his residence for the purpose of Campbell's studying and writing. It was here that Campbell wrote the *Declaration and Address*. This document has come to be known as the *Magna Charta* of the Restoration Movement.

It is a brilliant piece of religious thought, especially for that time, but it must not be considered a creed. This work is divided by three parts. The "Declaration" gives the purpose and plan for the Christian Association of Washington. The "Address" goes into detail of the forces at work in the religious world of that time. The third part, the "Appendix" is designed to answer questions, while refuting arguments pertaining to the Washington Association.

Alexander arrived with the rest of the family in New York on September 29, 1809. Thomas met them on their way to Washington, on October 19, and shared with Alexander the *Declaration and Address*. Little did he know that Alexander had reached many of the same conclusions while shipwrecked and living in Glasgow.

After reading the document, Alexander said that he would devote his life in preaching the principles his father had set forth. To which Thomas replied, "Upon these principles, my dear son, I fear you will have to wear many a ragged coat." Alexander preached his first sermon July 15, 1810. We will be having more to say about him as a preacher in the next lesson.

On May 4, 1811, the Christian Association of Washington decided to become an independent congregation. Thomas served as elder and Alexander served as its preacher. Normally, he would

21

preach for 1 ½ hours at home and three hours when visiting somewhere.

The small church constructed a new building to replace the temporary log building where they began. And because it was built in a brush run on the farm of William Gilchrist, both the building and the congregation became known as Brush Run Church, in Washington County, Pennsylvania.

The Question of Baptism: Sprinkling or Immersion?

Upon the birth of Alexander's first child, Jane (March 13, 1812), the question of infant sprinkling arose again. Alexander sought to study everything he could on the matter and found the practice to be lacking Bible example and authority. He immediately began making plans to be immersed. Joining him were his wife, sister, mother, and father. Some discrepancy exists among historians as to the number of people actually baptized that day. Some include James Foster and others do not. It is also believed that James and Sarah Henon were baptized that day. However, in time the whole congregation would be immersed.

The baptismal ceremony that day lasted for seven hours, with six hours of preaching on the subject leading up to the baptisms. Mathias Luce, a Baptist minister, baptized them. Seeing that Baptists were the only ones practicing immersion in that area, and their evident friendship, it seems reasonable that Alexander would ask him to do it. Campbell did however state that he would not be expressing a religious experience prior to baptism, as was a Baptist practice, but only his confession in Christ.

The Red Stone Association

It was not long until Alexander began receiving invitations to preach for the Baptists, and the Baptist "Red Stone Association" was seeking to add the little Brush Run congregation to their number. It seems likely that since the Baptists were not numerically strong in that region, and because the Brush Run congregation was believed to be "Baptist" in their practice of immersion, they should be part of that association. The church however had some reservations about what to do. Yet, believing that reform could be better accomplished from within an existing religious group than from without, the congregation agreed to join the association on the condition that they would be free from all creeds and permitted to continue studying the Bible and obeying God's commands wherever that took them. They were officially accepted to the association in 1813.

Alexander Campbell would later write about this, saying: "I had no idea of uniting with the Baptists more than with the Moravians or the mere Independents." Campbell regarded himself a Baptist only as far as immersion was concerned. Soon the union with the Redstone Association proved to be untenable. Campbell simply could not and would not agree with the *Philadelphia Confession of Faith,* the direct operation of the Holy Spirit on the heart of the sinner, baptism because sins were *already* forgiven, predestination unto eternal life, the notion of needing a religious experience prior to baptism, and the difference (or lack thereof in Baptist doctrine) between the Old and New Testaments.

When the association was scheduled to meet on August 30, 1816, Campbell was not originally asked to preach, but because the man scheduled to speak became ill, Campbell was invited to lecture. It was here that Campbell extemporaneously preached what has become his famous "Sermon on the Law." In his sermon, Campbell explained that the Law was fulfilled in Christ and at the cross, and was therefore not binding on Christians. His lessons caused tensions to mount increasingly between the Brush Run Church and the Redstone Association over the next few years.

Buffalo Seminary

In 1818, Campbell opened Buffalo Seminary in his home. His home was built by his father-in-law, John Brown, and was given to him along with 300 prime acres as an incentive to stay there and not move to Ohio as Campbell had desired. Needless to say, Campbell stayed.

Alexander later added a second edition to the home he would call "**Bethany**" in order to give it the necessary housing and classroom space needed for Buffalo Seminary. During the building, the Campbell family lived in the basement. The school opened in March of 1818 and closed four years later, due to a lack of interest among the young men in the area for the ministry.

Thomas Campbell, who was forbidden by Kentucky state law to teach black people, moved back to Pennsylvania and began teaching at the seminary in September of 1818.

The first of Alexander Campbell's debates occurred June 19-20, 1820. He debated a Presbyterian named John Walker in the Quaker community of Mt. Pleasant, Ohio (twenty-three miles from Bethany). The debate was on the subject of baptism. Walker's first speech was only two minutes long. Walker arrived the second day and requested that each disputant make only one speech. Campbell agreed to two speeches. Needless to say, Walker was not a debater and his brethren were not pleased with his effort (or lack thereof). This led to a second debate with the Presbyterians and W.L. McCalla in 1823.

Timeline of Events

- ➢ **1811** – The Brush Run Church is formed.
- ➢ **1812** – The Campbells are baptized, accepting immersion as the proper mode.
- ➢ **1816** – A. Campbell preaches his "Sermon on the Law."
- ➢ **1817** – Elias Smith announces his conversion to universalism.
- ➢ **1818** – Walter Scott arrives in America and in 1819 begins preaching a restoration plea.
- ➢ **1818** – A. Campbell opens Buffalo Seminary (T. Campbell is a teacher).
- ➢ **1820** – A. Campbell debates John Walker (Presbyterian) in Mt. Pleasant, Ohio.

Chapter Three

The Restoration Movement Gains Momentum

1821-1850

Alexander Campbell Meets Walter Scott

While living in Pittsburg, Walter Scott resided with the family of Nathaniel Richardson. Richardson was a wealthy merchant and had hired Scott to teach his son, Robert, and some of his friends, on Scott's condition that he would not teach them the Presbyterian Confession of Faith.

Alexander Campbell happened to be a close friend of the Richardson family. It was this friendship that led him to meet and develop a life-long friendship with Walter Scott.

The two met in the winter of 1821-22 and soon realized that they were both scholars of both New Testament Greek and Latin languages, and had both studied the works of Sandeman, the Haldane brothers, and John Locke. They both desired a return to the ancient order of the church and were willing to give themselves to advocating the restoration principles set forth in Thomas Campbell's *Declaration and Address.*

The similarities between these two men are astounding. Both were first-class biblical scholars. Both were respected educators. Scott served as president of Bacon College in Georgetown, Kentucky and Campbell was the founding president of Bethany College near his home. Both received a fine education and had been influenced by the learned reformers of Scotland. Both were gifted writers and careful editors. Both left a legacy in their writings and periodicals. Campbell's *Christian System* and Scott's *Gospel Restored* are both classic works. Both men were tremendous, even mesmerizing, preachers.

The Preaching of Walter Scott

Scott possessed an immense ability as an orator and expounder of the gospel. It was said of Scott that while preaching the parable of the prodigal son, one would think that the wayward young man was soon to enter their presence.

As an evangelist, he would come to be known as the "Golden Oracle." It was said that "his dark eyes seemed to penetrate the secrets of the soul." He would preach a simple, acceptable five-step plan of salvation: faith, repentance, baptism, remission of sins, and the gift of the Holy Spirit.

The Preaching of Alexander Campbell

General Robert E. Lee said of Alexander Campbell:

> "He was a man in whom were illustriously combined all the qualities that could adorn or elevate the nature to which he belonged; knowledge, the most various and extended, virtue that never loitered in her career nor deviated from her course. A man who, if he had been delegated a representative of his species to one of the many superior worlds, would have suggested a grand idea of the human race."

Campbell flourished as an evangelist. Unfortunately, only two or three of his sermons have been preserved. This is because he found the practice of writing sermons to be "exceedingly irksome and distasteful." It is hard to believe, but it appears that it did not occur to Campbell that others would want to read these sermons of his. Also, Campbell spoke extemporaneously. He did not speak from a manuscript, thus a manuscript would not have existed.

Of his preaching abilities, President James Madison said, "It was my pleasure to hear him very often as a preacher of the Gospel, and I regard him as the ablest and most original expounder of the Scriptures I have ever heard.

His style was his own. He did not intend to copy anyone. He hardly used any gesture or mannerism and had a great composure in the pulpit. He did not shout or get excited. His presence was calm and his tone conversational. Sometimes he would lean on his cane while standing and speak for two or three hours.

One tradition is that his students at Bethany would sometimes carry canes with them when they went out to preach. When he was older, he grew a long beard, thus prompting his students to do the same.

His enunciation was clear and distinct, chaste and simple. His sentences were clear and forceful. At times he would speak with utmost fervor, placing emphasis on key words and thoughts.

Campbell also gained national recognition as a debater. Let us note now the debates of Alexander Campbell.

Debates of Alexander Campbell

Campbell's first debate was with the Presbyterian **John Walker**. This debate took place in Mount Pleasant, Ohio on June 19-20, 1820. The debate was on the subject and mode of baptism.

On October 15-21, 1823, Campbell again debated a Presbyterian – **W.L. McCalla**. This debate was held in Washington, Kentucky and again the subject and mode of baptism was discussed. It was in this debate that Campbell introduced the scriptures which teach baptism for the remission of sins as a means of answering pedo-baptism.

These two debates convinced Campbell that "a week's debating is worth a year's preaching."

Campbell's third debate was with the atheist **Robert Owen**. This debate was held April 13-21, 1829 in Cincinnati, Ohio. The debate was held in the largest Methodist church building in the city and a former mayor of Cincinnati, Jacob Burnet, was one of the moderators. On the final day of the debate there were 1,200 present. During this debate Campbell gave an affirmative speech which lasted for 12 hours (2 sessions daily for 3 days). You can find this speech beginning with his 22nd reply in the written record of the debate. At the conclusion of the debate, Campbell asked those who favored Christianity to stand. All but three stood.

Campbell's next debate was with a Catholic Bishop named **John B. Purcell**. This debate took place in Cincinnati as well, lasting from January 13-21, 1837. In this debate Campbell argued against the immorality of the Catholic Church. Campbell showed from Catholic writing that a priest who might take a wife was to be excommunicated, but if he kept a "concubine" he was merely fined.

On November 15, 1843 a sixteen day debate commenced with another Presbyterian preacher, **Nathan L. Rice**. Henry Clay was the moderator. This debate was held in Lexington, Kentucky. Subjects discussed were baptism, creeds, and the operation of the Holy Spirit. When the Presbyterians began losing big numbers to the restoration right after its publication, they stopped publication of the written record, providing Campbell the opportunity to pick up the rights and continue to publish it.

Rice used most of Walker's and McCalla's arguments. Instead of 14 reasons why Baptism and circumcision differ, Campbell had 16. Campbell's greatest satisfaction from this debate came from the news that his Uncle Archibald in Ireland gave up infant baptism after reading it.

Campbell Leaves the Baptists

It is unfair to Campbell to say that he was ever truly a Baptist. The Baptists originally sought him because he was a gifted preacher who believed immersion was the only valid form of baptism.

Also, he lived in an area with very few Baptists and it appears they needed all the help they could get.

Campbell had no desire of joining any sect. However, neither did he desire to add a sect to the already existing sects pervading the land. He felt he could reform the Baptists and restore the pattern for the church from within their already existing framework. He was wrong. Although, he did help to bring a good many churches and preachers out of that denomination, he obviously failed to reform the whole.

In fact, Campbell was often embarrassed when he was acclaimed as being a great Baptist preacher. He would say time and again, "I have as much against you Baptists as I have against the Presbyterians" (the group he had previously left along with his father).

Separation with the Baptists became evident by 1830 with the dissolution of the Mahoning Association. John Henry made the motion to dissolve the association and Campbell, about to rise to his feet to oppose the motion, was hindered by the hand of Walter Scott upon his shoulder. The motion passed unanimously. These men had come to see that such an association lacked scriptural authority and wanted to take the restoration one step further. The fact that Campbell did not entirely agree with this motion, and his desire for continued cooperation among the churches, would eventually become a point of bitter controversy. In fact, Campbell was at a loss for direction. He asked, "Brethren, what now are you going to do? Are you never going to meet again?" It was then decided that they would continue to meet yearly, but not officially as an association.

After separation with the Baptists was complete, he would cease publishing the *Christian Baptist* and begin publishing the *Millennial Harbinger*.

The Men and Works of This Era

The simplicity and truthfulness of the Restoration Plea attracted many great preachers who were at the time questioning the denominational doctrines they had been "ordained" to preach. As our study of this period continues, let us begin by studying the lives and influences of a few of these great gospel preachers.

 **"Raccoon" John Smith** (1784-1868) is probably one of the most well-known and well-beloved preachers of the restoration. He surely endured his share of hardship. It is easy to love and appreciate this man for his love and attitude toward the Lord, His truth, and His church. He was a pivotal figure in the progress made toward uniting the Stone and Campbell groups.

Alexander Campbell said that brother Smith was the only man he knew that would have been ruined by an education. His lack of education was not due to a lack of desire, only a lack of opportunity in frontier East Tennessee and Kentucky.

His preaching was simple and directed to the common man. He would often preach for three hours – spending the first hour answering the errors of Calvinism, the second hour introducing the truth of the Bible, and the third hour exhorting people to obey.

John Smith was a Baptist preacher that studied himself out of Baptist doctrine and the Baptist Church. Having studied his way out of hard-shell Calvinism, he was able to instruct others of its errors. His work was done primarily in Kentucky. He "reformed" many Baptist churches and was quite controversial is doing so. Yet, he was so well-respected for his piety that it was hard for those who disagreed with him to dislike him. Perhaps he had the courage to ask the questions they were afraid to ask.

For Smith, the New Testament plainly revealed facts to be believed, commands to be obeyed, and promises to be enjoyed.

John Smith's Horse Hollow Cabin
(Monticello, KY)

Jacob Creath, Sr. (1777-1854) and his nephew **Jacob Creath, Jr.** (1799-1886) are also two great preachers who first had to leave the bonds of hard-shell Calvinism, along with John Smith. Like Smith, these men were renowned Baptist preachers in Kentucky. Also, like Smith, they began reading Alexander Campbell's *Christian Baptist*. They came to understand that the gospel could be obeyed, that creeds must be rejected, and that the church must be restored to its original faith and practice.

John T. Johnson (1788-1856) was more than the brother of Vice-President, Richard M. Johnson. He was a great preacher! He also loved the idea of Christian unity and left what could have been a very prosperous and prestigious political career to devote his life to the principles of the New Testament. He was also very instrumental in the founding of the missionary society.

34

John (1800-1867) **and Samuel** (1789-1877) **Rogers** were two brothers that made a significant contribution for the restoration in Kentucky and north of the Ohio River. The brothers were great gospel preachers and soul winners.

They had also learned their way out of Calvinism.

Benjamin Franklin (1812-1878), great-nephew of the statesman, was a very popular preacher and editor. Franklin was greatly influenced by John and Samuel Rogers. While living in Cincinnati, he started the *American Christian Review*. Franklin was a very conservative voice for New Testament Christianity and Christian unity. He opposed any doctrine, entity, or person he perceived to be divisive to the body of Christ.

T.M. Allen (1797-1871) was another of the great preachers of this era. He worked diligently to teach and covert souls in Missouri and in so doing helped to establish many churches in that state.

B.F. Hall (1803-1873) was a tremendous preacher in Kentucky, Tennessee, and later Texas. He was helped by reading the Campbell-McCalla debate and came to realize that baptism was for the remission of sins. He became a staunch defender of this truth and a great adversary to Calvinism.

Philip S. Fall (1798-1890) is best remembered for his evangelistic work in Kentucky and Tennessee. He helped to promote restoration principles among the Baptists in Nashville, which eventually led to the Baptist church denouncing its creed and Calvinism, and becoming the first church of Christ in that city. Fall was also considered a great educator for his time.

 **William Hayden** (1799-1863) was a companion of Walter Scott on the Western Reserve in present day Ohio. Scott would often preach his sermon and Hayden would conclude by exhorting the audience to respond. It is said that he had a "strong intellect, tender emotional nature, clear voice and fluent speech, he commanded attention at once and held it closely both in sermon and song. He was a logical reasoner, and pressed the claims of the gospel upon thinking men with convincing power and a pathos that was well-nigh irresistible."

Hayden preached for 35 years, traveled some 60,000 miles on horseback (90,000 in all), preached some 9,000 sermons, and baptized 1,200 souls. For 25 years he averaged being away from home 240 nights per year.

Jesse B. Ferguson (1819-1870) was a very brilliant and popular preacher, and he knew it. Some claim that he was spoiled by the compliments that he received and the praises which were given him. Ferguson went into Universalism and spiritualism. He was so popular that he carried a very large per-  centage of the church in Nashville with him. Many other churches in Tennessee were affected by his teaching.

From April – June 1852 Jesse B. Ferguson incited controversy with the Nashville congregation beginning with an article teaching a second chance for forgiveness after death and culminating with an article stating his disbelief in eternal punishment. During this time a beautiful new church building was built.

On June 1, 1856, Jesse B. Ferguson finally resigned his ministry at the Nashville congregation at the threat of a law suit. In 1852, the church at Nashville is said to have numbered 550 members. By the time of Ferguson's resignation, the church numbered less than 200. On April 8, 1857, the new building built for the Nashville congregation mysteriously burned to the ground.

The church would have to move back into its old building and hire its former preacher, Philip S. Fall to bring stability to the congregation, which he did. Fall would stay until 1877.

Brotherhood Periodicals from This Era

The *Christian Baptist* was Alexander Campbell's first periodical. It was published from 1823-1830 and has been considered an iconoclastic paper. Campbell even admitted that he was using this paper as a means of testing whether or not people were willing and desirous of religious reform. Walter Scott helped him in editing this paper.

The *Christian Messenger* was Barton W. Stone's paper which began in 1826 and continued until close to his death in 1844. He hoped Christian unity would be the "polar star" of this work. John T. Johnson helped him for a while as an associate editor.

The *Evangelist* was a paper Walter Scott began publishing in 1832. It was postponed for a while in 1835 in favor of writing his great book, *The Gospel Restored*, which was published in 1836. *The Evangelist* was resumed in 1836 and finally ceased forever in 1842.

The *Millennial Harbinger* was Alexander Campbell's second and final periodical. Campbell chose to drop the name of the *Christian Baptist* and use this name after he had officially separated from the Baptists.

This work ran from 1830-1870, although Campbell only served as its editor until 1865 when W.K. Pendleton (his son-in-law) became editor.

Campbell was a post-millennial theorist, meaning that he believed Christ would return after 1,000 prosperous years for the church. He also believed the work he was doing was going to help begin that 1,000 year period.

The *Christian Review* was Tolbert Fanning's paper. This paper ran from 1844-1847. It was replaced by Jesse B. Ferguson's *Christian Magazine.* Fanning also edited a couple of science and agricultural journals. His most notable paper, however, was the *Gospel Advocate* which began in July of 1855.

The *Reformer* (1846) and later the *American Christian Review* was Benjamin Franklin's paper. The *ACR* began in 1856 and continued until his death in 1878.

In the December 1835 issue of the *Millennial Harbinger*, a list of brotherhood periodicals was given. In addition to those we have mentioned, there were also the following: *Apostolic Advocate* (John Thomas, Richmond, VA); *Gospel Advocate* (J.T. Johnson and Dr. Hall, Georgetown, KY); *Primitive Christian* (Silas E. Shepherd, Auburn, NY); *Christian Investigator* (William Hunter, Eastport, ME); *The Christian Preacher* (D.S. Burnett, Cincinnati, OH); *The Christian Reformer* (John R. Howard, Paris, TN); and *The Disciple* (James A. Butler and A. Graham, Alabama).

Unity between Stone and Campbell

In 1830 two predominant groups were seeking to restore New Testament Christianity in America. Barton W. Stone and his friends were seeking to restore the faith in Kentucky, Tennessee, Ohio, Indiana, and Illinois. They went by the name "Christian," and were typically known as Christian Churches or churches of Christ.

Thomas and Alexander Campbell, along with Walter Scott and John Smith were seeking to restore the faith among Baptists primarily in Ohio, Kentucky, Pennsylvania, and what is now West Virginia. They were usually called "Reformers" or "Disciples."

Having left the Baptists, unity between Stone and Campbell could be realized. Unity between the two groups of Stone and Campbell, however, would have to come over the course of time.

Campbell's 1823 debate with W.L. MacCalla in the state of Kentucky, where the Stone group was strong, certainly helped lay some of the groundwork for unity. Campbell was received so well by Kentucky Baptists that he scheduled a three month preaching tour the following year. While on this tour Campbell and Stone met for the first time in Georgetown, Kentucky. Soon the *Christian Baptist* had a large circulation in Kentucky and many Baptists came to accept the views of restoration which Stone had been preaching in their home state.

Congregations of the two groups began to extend fellowship to one another and some eventually merged. The first such merger occurred in Millersburg, Kentucky on April 24, 1831. The two groups agreed that they were one as far as faith and practice was concerned and decided to meet together as one congregation.

Another development that helped to aid unity was for the brethren of the two groups to work together on joint projects. For example, Walter Scott and Joseph Gaston worked together as traveling evangelists in the Western Reserve of Ohio. Also, Stone conducted a gospel meeting in November, 1831 at the Great Crossings congregation where John T. Johnson was the minister. John T.

Johnson would later serve as the associate editor of Stone's paper *The Christian Messenger.*

"Raccoon" John Smith and John Rogers joined with Stone and Johnson in a series of unity discussions. The four men decided to call a general meeting to discuss unity at Georgetown, Kentucky on December 23-26, 1831. A second meeting was conducted over the New Year's weekend in Lexington, Kentucky. Smith was the spokesman for the Campbell group and, after having pled for unity, concluded by saying:

> "Let us, then, my brethren, be no longer Campbellites or Stoneites, New Lights or Old Lights, or any other kind of lights, but let us come to the Bible and to the Bible alone, as the only book in the world that can give us all the light we need."

On this basis he and Stone extended the right hand of fellowship to symbolize the unity of the two groups.

It's very significant to our discussion to realize that unity was achieved *because* of doctrine and not *despite* it. It's amazing to consider that these two groups shared so much in common because of their "back to the Bible" approach, even without having a great deal of contact and familiarity with one another.

Bill Humble cites the following six similarities in his book "The Story of the Restoration" pp.31-32.

1.) Both groups accepted the Bible as the sole rule for faith and practice – rejecting creeds etc.

2.) Both pleaded for Christian unity on the basis of a return to the Bible.

3.) Both denied Calvinistic teachings such as limited atonement, predestination, and total depravity. They believed the gospel should be preached to every man and that any man could accept it.

4.) Both rejected infant sprinkling and accepted immersion of believers as the only scriptural form of baptism.

5.) Both refused to wear unscriptural and sectarian names.

6.) Both regarded denominational organizations such as presbyteries, synods, and ruling associations as unscriptural.

However, the two groups also had their differences. Humble cites the following four:

1.) They disagreed about names. Stone's group believed the name "Christian" was the name given by God and superseded all others (on the basis of Acts 11:26). Campbell believed they should wear the name "disciples." Both names continued to be used even after the Lexington meeting.

2.) They differed on the emphasis placed on baptism. Stone's group had yet to conclude that baptism was essential for the remission of sins, although some of them had begun so teaching. Also, Stone believed the church could fellowship those who had yet to be immersed while Campbell did not. **(In all of these things, however, it matters not what Stone or Campbell said, but what the Bible says. See Mark 16:16, Acts 2:38, Acts 22:16, 1 Peter 3:21.)**

3.) Stone's group had not been practicing weekly observance of the Lord's Supper as had Campbell's. Unity was eventually achieved on this issue on the basis of such passages as 1 Corinthians 11:17 ff. The churches of Christ continue to observe the Lord's Supper every first day of the week when we come together into one place.

4.) Stone's group also placed more of an emphasis on the Holy Spirit's working in conversion than Campbell's group did. Campbell's approach was more logical than emotional. He emphasized the role of reason in conversion while Stone emphasized the role of emotion.

Following the Lexington meeting, John Smith and John Rogers traveled throughout Kentucky urging brethren in every community where two congregations existed to become one. Barton W. Stone said of this union, "This union...I view as the noblest act of my life."

Results of Unity

With a united front, numerical growth was inevitable. The decade of the 1830's saw incredible increases in the numbers of the local churches and the work being accomplished. At least 28 journals were published during the 1830's, the most notable being Campbell's *Millennial Harbinger* (1830), Scott's *Evangelist* (1832), while Stone's *Christian Messenger* (1826) continued growing.

The 1830's saw the founding of the first college associated with the movement – **Bacon College**. Bacon College began in Georgetown, Kentucky in 1836 with Walter Scott serving as its first president. Campbell began **Bethany College** on his home-place in 1840, while Tolbert Fanning opened **Franklin College** north of Nashville, Tennessee in 1845.

The growth of the church was phenomenal and it was marked by solid, expository preaching. It has been said that the preachers of this era relied solely on their Bibles, knowing little about philosophy.

By 1836, D.S. Burnett documented that the church numbered over 100,000 and ranked as the fourth largest religious body in America.

By 1850 another man cited in the *Ecclesiastical Reformer* that the church numbered 200,000 strong, while others believed the number to be as high as 300,000.

Timeline of Events 1821-1850

➤ **January 20, 1822**: Alexander Campbell meets Walter Scott.

➤ **December 1822**: Campbell closes Buffalo Seminary.

➤ **August 3, 1823**: Campbell begins the *Christian Baptist*.

➤ **August 31, 1823**: Campbell forms a congregation near his home at Wellsburg.

➤ **October 15-21 1823:** The Campbell – McCalla debate occurs.

➤ **1824:** Stone and Campbell meet for the first time.

➤ **Spring 1826:** Campbell publishes the *Living Oracles*.

➤ **November 25, 1826:** Barton W. Stone begins publishing the *Christian Messenger.*

➤ **March 1827:** Walter Scott begins his work as a traveling evangelist for the Mahoning Association

➤ **April 13-21, 1829**: Campbell – Owen debate

➤ **May 1829**: Buffalo (later named Bethany) congregation is formed by Thomas and Alexander Campbell.

➤ **January 4, 1830:** Alexander Campbell begins publishing the *Millennial Harbinger*.

➤ **December 23, 1831 – January 2, 1832:** Unity meetings take place in Georgetown and Lexington, Kentucky between the Stone and Campbell groups.

➤ **January 2, 1832:** Walter Scott begins publishing the *Evangelist*.

➤ **November 10, 1836:** Students arrive for classes at Bacon College in Georgetown, Kentucky. This is the first college of the movement and Walter Scott is the unanimous selection for president.

➤ **January 13-21, 1837**: Campbell – Purcell debate

➤ **March 2, 1840:** Bethany College founded

➤ **November 15, 1843:** Campbell – Rice debate begins

➤ **January 1, 1845**: Franklin College is opened by Tolbert Fanning.

➤ **May 4, 1847:** Campbell leaves America for a preaching tour of England, Scotland, and Ireland. He returns on October 19, and receives word of the death of his son Wycliffe.

➤ **October 23, 1849:** Meeting begins in Cincinnati, Ohio to discuss the formation of a missionary society.

Chapter Four

The American Christian Missionary Society

Alexander Campbell's Role in the ACMS

Alexander Campbell wanted to initiate more congregational co-operation in the realm of evangelism. He did not believe the local church working in and of itself was sufficient to the task.

Campbell also believed that for cooperation to be realized a new organization, similar to that of the Baptist associations was needed. As Lot's wife looked back to Sodom and Gomorrah, Campbell looked back on his days among the Baptists and began promoting an idea for a departmentalized form of church government.

According to his plan, churches would be divided into sections according to counties, districts, and even states. The organizations would have authority to send out preachers, pay them, ordain them, discipline them, and even discipline unruly churches! His plans for district organization prompted Walter Scott to ask, "Who made brother Campbell an organizer over us?" Strange as it may seem, Scott was the one who would later suggest the title: American Christian Missionary Society. He also wrote in defense and support of the society and was one of the first vice-presidents (there were twenty in all).

Campbell also used his editorial pen effectively and steadfastly. Though his ideas were met initially with resistance, they eventually won more and more favor as Campbell continued to write about organization and cooperation.

Clearly, brethren wanted to see more of an effort being made in evangelism, but were not sure how to make this effort scriptural. Campbell introduced the argument of expediency and argued that no scriptural command or example was evident to serve as a pattern for church action. Churches began holding cooperative meetings and forming associations to send out preachers in their area.

The Role of D.S. Burnett

 **D.S. Burnett** (1808-1867), son of the one-time mayor of Cincinnati, is best remembered for the role he played in the founding of the American Christian Bible Society and the American Christian Missionary Society.

Burnett's pro-Union stance alienated many brethren in the South before, during, and after the Civil War. Many southern Christians began the view the ACMS as an auxiliary for pro-Union politics.

Burnett was instrumental in the effort for a missionary society, being is responsible for beginning the American Christian Bible Society on January 27, 1845. The Bible society did not last, however, as it was terminated by the Ohio State Convention in 1856.

In the late spring of 1849, Campbell began to urge brethren to set a time and location for a brotherhood-wide meeting to discuss a plan for universal evangelism. Ironically enough, Campbell continued to press during the summer of 1849 for a "more efficient and **scriptural** organization."

Over time, Campbell and D.S. Burnett would bring to fruition this brotherhood-wide meeting. The date for the meeting was set for October 23, 1849 in Cincinnati and coincided with the annual meeting of the Bible society. Campbell, who was at first opposed to the Bible society, did not want these two meetings to coincide. Thus, he did not attend the meeting he had been urging (although he did send his son-in-law, W.K. Pendleton). It was claimed that Campbell was sick, but he was known to have carried on his other duties during that time.

Even though he was absent from the proceedings, Campbell was elected as president. D.S. Burnett and 19 others were elected vice-presidents. The role of officers reads like a virtual "Who's Who" among the preachers of that time.

Opponents to the Missionary Society

Tolbert Fanning (1810-1872) was one of the most important opponents of the missionary society. He lived in the Nashville area and was the most influential preacher in the South during the 1850's and 1860's. He was the founder of Franklin College, and founding-editor of the *Gospel Advocate* (1855). In fact, his primary purpose for the *Gospel Advocate* was to examine the subjects of church organization and church cooperation.

Fanning believed the scriptural way to conduct mission work was through the local church. He believed one church could commission a man to go and preach the gospel while asking for financial support from sister congregations. He stated that this method had "the authority of Scriptural examples."

In 1859 Fanning was invited to the missionary society's annual convention to lecture on the mission work being conducted by Tennessee congregations. He took this opportunity to explain to them how the churches in Tennessee were working together to establish congregations among the Cherokee Indians without the aid of a missionary society. While Fanning did make his objections known, he concluded by saying, "But I am happy to say, that from what I have heard on this floor, we are one people. With us all there is one faith, one God, one body and one spirit." Things would soon change.

Benjamin Franklin (1812-1878) became a strong opponent of the missionary society after the Civil War. He was the most popu-

50

lar preacher in the brotherhood during the 1860's and 1870's. He edited the most influential journal after the Civil War in the *American Christian Review* (1856). His debates have also been considered as some of the best since the debates of Alexander Campbell.

Needless to say, Benjamin Franklin exerted a tremendous influence among his brethren. He had not always been an opponent of the missionary society. In fact, he was at the first convention in 1849. He had held one office or another for 17 consecutive years beginning in 1850, including the most important office of the society which was that of corresponding secretary (1856-1857).

He was a supporter and defender of the society until the society adopted a resolution in favor of the Union in 1863. Franklin did not support the War and urged Christians not to fight in it. He believed this resolution in favor of the union brought "strife and contention" to the church and he was right. In 1866, Franklin announced that he no longer supported the society and believed it to be an unscriptural organization. He held this position and fought against the society until his death in 1878.

David Lipscomb (1831-1917) followed Fanning as the editor of the *Gospel Advocate* in 1868, after having served for two years with Fanning as co-editor. He had been a student of Fanning's at Franklin College and also a faculty member. Lipscomb continued to edit the *Advocate* for more than 45 years and during those years he had a greater influence on churches in the South than any other man.

Some pro-society brethren charged that anyone who did not support such an effort did so simply because they lacked the necessary zeal for good works. That theory is utterly demolished by casually surveying the life of David Lipscomb. Not only was he a great preacher, he was a great writer and editor. He poured his life-blood into projects like the *Gospel Advocate*, Fanning Orphan School (c.1884), and the Nashville Bible School (c.1891), which is now called Lipscomb University in Nashville, Tennessee. He opposed the society, not because he was a do-nothing, but because he believed it to be an unscriptural organization. His worry was that such bodies would rob the church of her purpose and cause the church to become "an empty, meaningless form .... [where] its authority and usefulness are gone forever."

In 1867 Lipscomb had a written debate with Thomas Munnell on the propriety of the missionary society. Lipscomb had argued that 10,000 churches could cooperate in a scriptural way without any missionary society. Munnell rebutted that he wanted Lipscomb to describe how that many churches could work together in a business-like way. Lipscomb's reply follows:

> "We do not know that God proposed to convert the world in a business-like way. Wise men, intent on the accomplishment of a great object, would scarcely choose a babe, born out of wedlock, cradled in a manger, as the efficient superintendent in the accomplishment of that work. Business men would have hardly sought out unlearned, simple hearted fishermen as their agents, would not have chosen the infamy of the Cross, and the degradation of the grave. This is so un-business like that, business men, entering in strive to change it to a more business-like manner....God's ways are not man's ways, for the foolishness of God is wiser than man."

Lipscomb is best remembered for his child-like faith in God's word and a resolute conviction in the authority of that word.

The American Civil War and Christian Pacifism

By 1860, the church had some 2,000 congregations – 1,200 in the North and 800 in the South.

Except for Walter Scott, all the early leaders of the church had been pacifists. Moreover, at the beginning of the Civil War the majority of preachers and editors urged non-participation on the basis that "brother should not go to war with brother." It appears that most preachers and editors were against brethren going to war or even declaring sides politically.

J.W. McGarvey (1829-1911) wrote, "I would rather, ten thousand times, be killed for refusing to fight than to fall in battle, or come home victorious with the blood of my brethren on my hands." The issue for many was not whether warfare was wrong, or whether or not the government could wield a sword, but whether a Christian should go to war knowing that he would be called upon to kill a brother in Christ. McGarvey asked his brethren what the twelve apostles would have done had they been living during the Civil War. He wondered if they would have lined up on opposite sides for battle, or urged their brethren to enlist.

Tolbert Fanning suffered greatly to see many of his students leave the school to enlist in the Confederate Army. At least twenty graduates entered the Confederate forces as commissioned officers. One faculty member, Pierce Butler Anderson, a graduate of West Point and distinguished veteran of the Mexican War, left to become an artillery captain under General Robert E. Lee.

A number of brethren also enlisted with the Union Army, such as future United States President **James A. Garfield**. Garfield was

 the president of Western Reserve Eclectic Institute in Hiram, Ohio at the outset of the war. He petitioned the governor of Ohio to give him an appointment in the Union Army. He was commissioned as a Lieutenant-Colonel and was given permission to raise a regiment. He did so by returning to Hiram and raising a unit even from among the young men of his student body. He formed the 42nd regiment of the Ohio Volunteer Infantry.

Garfield was soon made a full colonel and was given full command of the regiment. This group fought for General Grant at Shiloh and then in Corinth, Mississippi. Garfield was then assigned to General Rosecrans at Murfreesboro, Tennessee and was with him at Chattanooga and Chickamauga. After reaching the rank of Brigadier-General, Garfield resigned to enter Congress as a representative from Ohio.

T.B. Larimore (1843-1929) was also at Shiloh. In fact, it was Larimore who wrote the dispatch that went to Confederate General Albert Sydney Johnson, notifying him of the passage of the first Federal gunboat up the river. Larimore was captured while stationed in the Sequatchie Valley of east Tennessee. He took a "noncombatant oath" and returned home.

T.B. Larimore was a person seemingly loved by all in the brotherhood. He did not take a stand either way on the controversial issues of the day. His answer was that he simply did not know what the Lord taught on the subject of the instrument. Nevertheless, he was a great preacher. For more information on Larimore, see *The Man from Mars Hill*, by J.M. Powell.

Larimore was educated by Tolbert Fanning at Franklin College. He went on to establish his own school in Florence, Alabama, titled Mars Hill Academy (January 1, 1871). Later the school grew to be Mars Hill College. This school continued from 1871 to 1887 when Larimore decided to devote himself fully to preaching. E.A. Elam taught for a while with him there. It is believed that this college did more for young people in that section of the country than all other schools there.

The man who preached the night Tolbert Fanning was baptized, B.F. Hall, became a sadistic chaplain in the Confederate Army. He served in a regiment of Texas Rangers which was led by Barton Stone, son of Barton W. Stone. Hall advocated cutting off the right hand of any captured Union soldier and sending them back north with the dismembered hand attached to their saddlebag. Hall died believing Fanning was his enemy because Fanning criticized this attitude. Hall never again held the level of influence he held before the war.

David Lipscomb played a primary role in urging brethren to remain pacifists. Lipscomb was a powerful preacher and a genuinely good man. In Nashville, his influence lasted for generations. Truly this type of man comes only so often and when he does, mankind should take notice.

On one occasion Nathan Bedford Forrest sent a member of his staff to hear Lipscomb preach in Columbia, Tennessee, suspecting he might be a Union sympathizer. The staff officer was moved to tears on several occasions by the sermon. He concluded that he could not tell for certain whether or not Lipscomb was loyal to the Confederacy, but he knew he was certainly loyal to Christ.

While these men were staunch pacifists, the brotherhood also had some very staunch abolitionists. Throughout the 1850's some preachers cried out for slavery to be denounced and slave-owning brethren to be dis-fellowshipped.

Believing that Alexander Campbell was soft on the slavery issue, these men began a rival college in Indianapolis called Northwestern Christian University. It is now known as Butler University.

The worst thing that could have happened did, when in 1861 and 1863 the American Christian Missionary Society took a political stand and sided with the Union. This action caused pacifistic brethren in the North and South to feel betrayed by the society. Previous supporters such as McGarvey, Franklin, and Moses E. Lard turned against the society for its political involvement in the war.

After the war Lipscomb stated, "We felt, we still feel, that the Society committed a great wrong against the Church and cause of God. We have felt, we still feel, that without evidence of a repentance of the wrong, it should not receive the confidence of the Christian brotherhood."

 **Robert Milligan** (1814-1875) was the president of Bacon College in Kentucky, which after it merged with Transylvania College in Lexington became Kentucky University. It was the only college in Kentucky that remained open throughout the war. He also was a pacifist. Milligan gave us such works as *The Scheme of Redemption* and *Reason and Revelation*.

Tolbert Fanning and Benjamin Franklin used their respective papers to urge brethren not to enlist. Both men felt strongly about their respective governments, but considered the unity of the brotherhood a far greater prize.

The Resolutions of the Missionary Society

The following is taken from Jimmy Cutter, *Old Paths Advocate* (April, May, and June 1986).

Despite such pleas for political abstinence, in the first wartime meeting of the American Christian Missionary Society at Cincinnati on October 22-24, 1861, while churches from the South were not represented, Dr. John P. Robison introduced the resolution stating they were "deeply sympathetic" with the "present efforts to sustain the Government of the United States." He continued, "We feel it our duty as Christians, to ask our brethren everywhere to do all in their power to sustain the proper and constitutional authorities of the Union."

After considerable discussion a recess was called for a mass meeting, after which a short speech was delivered by James A. Garfield wearing a Union officer's uniform. The resolution was accepted with only one negative vote. Franklin later wrote that many of the delegates would have opposed the recess if they had known its purpose; not because they opposed the resolution, but because they opposed "introducing it into our missionary meeting." Franklin said Alexander Campbell and W. K. Pendleton sat in silence through the "political meeting" because they looked on it "as a farce."

Fanning informed his readers that the Society had "passed strong resolutions, approving most heartily of the wholesale murder of the people" in the South. The Society was encouraging "professed servants to cut the throats of their southern brethren." Fanning wondered how such men could ever again associate with the southern Christians "for whose blood they are now thirsting. Without thorough repentance, and abundant works demonstrating it, we cannot see how we can ever regard preachers who enforce political opinions by the sword, in any other light than monsters of intention, if not in very deed."

Although Fanning had been opposing the Society for nearly a decade and had led most southern Christians to accept his views, he could call them "one people" in 1859. Now the same leaders were "monsters" who could not be "fraternized as brethren."

On the other hand, many northern Christians felt that the refusal of the Society to adopt a pro-Union resolution without recessing for a mass meeting hinted at disloyalty to the Union. Abolitionists led by John Boggs, Pardee, and Ovid Butler, had organized a rival anti-slavery Christian Missionary Society. They demanded that the older American Christian Missionary Society adopt a forthright resolution denouncing slavery and supporting the North as a payment for their disbanding their rival Society.

When the Society met again in 1863, R. Faurot offered a strong resolution stating that God ordained powers and they were to be subject to them, and that "an armed rebellion exists, subversive of these divine injunctions."

Since reports had gone abroad that the Society was partially disloyal to the Union, they stated "we unqualifiedly declare allegiance to the said government." It was further resolved they tenderly sympathized with "our brave and noble soldiers in the field, who are defending us from the attempts of armed traitors to overthrow the Government." The vote on the resolution had few dissenters.

There were northern Christians who warned that Christians should stay out of the war controversy. Franklin said while "mistaken brethren may pass resolutions till doomsday," such actions would hinder the work rather than further it. Later when he denounced all missionary societies as unscriptural he pointed to the

1863 loyalty resolution as an important factor in changing his position.

The loyalty resolution also brought stern protests from J. W. McGarvey and Moses E. Lard. McGarvey said most Christians accepted the Societies as expedients but the test of a society was its usefulness. Whenever it presumed to speak on matters of faith or occasioned strife in the church it should be abandoned, and: "By the above standards I have judged the American Christian Missionary Society, and have decided for myself, that it should now cease to exist."

Moses E. Lard's criticisms were similar to Franklin's. He believed that a society should do "absolutely nothing" except spread the gospel. Lard called the 1863 loyalty resolution "a mournful and humiliating" example of an unwarranted assumption of power. Lard was willing to give the Society a chance to correct this mistake but if it ever again adopted a political resolution it should die.

However, the Society did adopt another political resolution. When the war ended, the 1865 Society meeting moved to thank God for the emancipation of four million slaves, the return of peace, and the opportunity for missionary work in their own border. Therefore it was resolved that they gratefully "accept the leadings of Providence, and will endeavor to meet the exigency, that the poor may have the gospel preached to them." An earlier draft of the resolution was much sharper.

Along with this resolution the board's Annual Report called for a renewing of fellowship with the southern Christians. Despite the deep flow of human blood that included a murdered President they said "we can well afford to extend men the right hand of fellowship to each other, without regard to dividing lines."

The Missionary Society's records furnish strong evidence that the impact of the Civil War was divisive. When the Board of Managers presented the annual report in 1879 they admitted that the Society had been compelled to fight against four forces. Heading the list were the "alienations produced by the late war."

Division between North and South Following the War

The division between churches in the North and South did not come simply because of the Civil War. Granted, if there had been no war, a great many things would have been avoided. Yet, this division between churches in the North and South was as much doctrinal as anything else.

The churches in the South typically were more conservative than the churches in the North. The southern congregations generally opposed mechanical instruments and the missionary society. Also, the journals being published and circulated throughout the South had no "progressive" agenda.

The division between northern and southern congregations grew sharper over the next generation and is still evident today.

Chapter Five

Division Strikes the Church

1851-1900

Within 60 years (1810-1870) the church had grown to at least 350,000 members in 2,800 congregations and was one of the five largest religious bodies in America.

The majority of congregations were in the North. States like Ohio, Indiana, Illinois, and Missouri were strong regions for New Testament Christianity. However, many areas in these states today are considered mission fields.

The decade of the **1850's** was one of opposition to the newly formed American Christian Missionary Society. The decade of the **1860's** was marked by division over the issue of Civil War. The decade of the **1870's** was marked by controversy surrounding the use of mechanical instruments of music in worship. Also, during this period the movement lost some of its valuable leaders, while gaining some others. Thus, Satan struck during a leadership transition period.

The period of 1871-1900 was one of transition for the church. Two differing sides emerged and stood firmly entrenched in their convictions and were philosophically opposed to one another. The period began with an imminent division looming and ended with two bodies, where once there stood only one. By the end of this period, the unity Stone, Campbell, Smith, and others delighted to see had been replaced with bitter discord, a lasting division, many lessons learned, and many lessons unlearned.

Amazingly, even though brethren differed bitterly in their beliefs on missionary societies and instrumental music, the period leading up to the division of the 1890's was one of phenomenal growth. The time was ripe for growth. The war had people searching for God and the poverty-stricken Southland was searching for hope.

By the year 1880, the little group of 29 that had begun at Brush Run, and the small little number of disciples Stone had amassed in Kentucky, had grown to number approximately 563,928. The church consisted of approximately 4,768 congregations and employed an estimated 3,488 preachers.

By the census of 1906, the combined number rose to 1,142,359 members in 10,942 congregations. Of this number, 982,701 members in 8,293 churches called themselves the Christian Church or Disciples, while 159,685 members in 2,649 congregations were known as the churches of Christ. Just think of what might have been accomplished had there been no division.

James A. Garfield Becomes President

James Garfield was elected as the 20th President of the United States in 1881, after nine terms in the U.S. House of Representatives. His Presidency was impactful, but cut short after 200 days when he was assassinated.

Earl West said of Garfield's presidency, "For strength of moral character and devotion to God the presidency has never known Garfield's equal." (*Search for the Ancient Order*, vol. 2, p.220)

Garfield's success in politics added fuel to the ongoing brotherhood debate on the Christian's role in civil government. Lipscomb asked, if Garfield's decision was acceptable, why not have all young men of similar ability to forsake the ministry for law, war, and politics?

Others attempted to convince Lipscomb that without Christians in civil government, governments would be run by heathens, but this had little avail.

Nevertheless, the great tragedy of Garfield's death helped to bring a broken America back together in much the same way that a death in the family might bring estranged relatives together again.

The Passing of a Generation

In Kentucky, the church owes a debt of gratitude to four outstanding evangelists who built upon the courage of Barton W. Stone (1772-1844). These men are John T. Johnson (1788-1856), "Raccoon" John Smith (1784-1868), Jacob Creath Sr. (1777-1854), and Jacob Creath, Jr. (1799-1886).

In Virginia and Ohio the church grew because of the preaching of men like Thomas Campbell (1763-1854), Alexander Campbell (1788-1866), Walter Scott (1796-1861), and William Hayden (1799-1863) to name a few.

You will observe that this period of restoration history saw the passing of all of these men. The brotherhood, however, still had some outstanding leaders. Whenever a "Moses" falls, a "Joshua" must arise. The brotherhood still had great men of wisdom and experience to lead them. Men like Benjamin Franklin and Jacob Creath, Jr., Philip S. Fall and Tolbert Fanning; these assumed the mantle of leadership. Also, a group of new leaders emerged which would determine the course of restoration history from that time onward.

New Leaders Emerge

During this period J.W. McGarvey (1829-1911) was hitting his stride as a leader in the church. He wrote his first *Commentary on Acts* at age 33 (1863) and revised it in 1892. During this time he also wrote: *Lands of the Bible, Evidences of Christianity, Jesus and Jonah, The Eldership, A Guide to Bible Study, A Commentary on*

Matthew and Mark, McGarvey's Sermons, and *McGarvey's Class Notes.*

In addition to his writing books, he edited the *Apostolic Times* (1869-1876) and beginning January 7, 1893 he wrote a column for the *Christian Standard* titled, "Biblical Criticism" which was later bound in book form.

McGarvey also taught at and headed the College of the Bible in Lexington, Kentucky. McGarvey, Robert Graham (1822-1901), and I.B. Grubbs (1833-1912) formed the nucleus that made this school great for many years. However, the liberalism they fought to their death prevailed in the College after they had passed. Today it is one of the most liberal seminaries a person could attend.

For a while the College of the Bible was a separate entity and not associated with Kentucky University. But it was again incorporated as part of Kentucky University in 1878. C.L. Loos served as President of KU during this time, while McGarvey was over the College of the Bible.

John William McGarvey spoke and wrote strongly against the use of instrumental music in worship in the beginning of the controversy, but it was during this period that he began to focus more on the theological liberalism and rationalism creeping into the church. He believed instrumental music in worship was just a fashion of the day and would soon pass. Moreover, he did not believe he had been very persuasive in changing minds on the subject. It's interesting to consider whether he may have given up too soon.

Isaac Errett, W.K. Pendleton, W.T. Moore, L.L. Pinkerton, Robert Richardson, and a few others formed the nucleus for the leadership of the progressive movement.

 **W.K. Pendleton** (1817-1899) was twice the son-in-law of Alexander Campbell. He succeeded Campbell as the editor of the *Millennial Harbinger* and as president of Bethany College. He was not as conservative as Campbell and under his direction Bethany College began to move somewhat away from the facts of the gospel into the realm of theological speculation.

"Progressiveness" was a philosophy put into practice. They believed in the *spirit* of the law more than the *letter*. To them, this philosophy applied to matters of church organization, mission work, worship, and even the basic question of who was a Christian.

The ranks of the progressive movement would swell in the coming years and their words became bolder. This philosophy led many brethren to believe all that was required to be saved was to have a pious character.

The divisiveness of these men led to two bodies being polarized in the churches of Christ and the Christian Church. Tragically, the unity and fellowship between Stone and Campbell would be wasted.

The "Progressive" Movement and the Instrument

Isaac Errett began publishing the *Christian Standard* with the help of a few brethren like James A. Garfield and W.K. Pendleton believing that the church needed a "more progressive religion" and sought to influence such change through the pen and the pulpit.

Dr. L.L. Pinkerton of Midway, Kentucky was also part of the "progressive" movement in the church. Pinkerton admitted that as far as he knew, he was the only preacher among the churches in

Kentucky that advocated the use of the instrument in worship. Around 1860 he and the church at Midway began using mechanical instruments of music, attempting to justify it on the basis of their poor singing. By 1868, it is believed that only 50 congregations used mechanical instruments in worship.

The first time this issue was discussed at length in a brotherhood paper was in the 1864-1865 issues of the *Millennial Harbinger*. By this time W.K. Pendleton had become the editor, succeeding Alexander Campbell. He argued that the use of the instrument was a matter merely of expediency. Men like J.W. McGarvey, Moses E. Lard, and Benjamin Franklin opposed its use. After McGarvey's death in 1911, an organ was used in his funeral service. One elderly lady commented, "This is a great wrong, for he opposed it all his life."

The church building in Cincinnati also became a point of controversy during these years. In February, 1872, the church in Cincinnati moved into their new $140,000 church building and worshiped with an $8,000 organ. It featured the largest stained glass window in America. This building was far from the simple structures that had been built up to that time. Brethren were alarmed at its costs and judged it to be a "temple of folly and pride." Thus, the Cincinnati building became another sore spot between conservative and progressive brethren.

In this case, we see something that is expedient to assembling together, a church building, believed to have been mishandled in poor judgment. Sometimes people will conflict in what they believe to be matters of good and poor judgment, as was the case here.

The Foreign Missionary Society came to replace the American Christian Missionary Society during this time. In 1869, the ACMS, led by Errett, instituted the "Louisville Plan" in which missionary boards were set up at the district, state, and national levels. The plan was for each level to kick 50% of their funds to the next highest level. It proved, however, to be a dismal failure. A new society, using the original plan, was established in 1875 by Isaac Errett and W.T. Moore.

The Leaven of the Progressives

A pervading doctrine among the progressives during this time was that the New Testament spoke only to sinners. They believed the New Testament held no instruction for saints, and thus the church was free to do whatever it pleased. This became a popular doctrine at Bethany College, and was one reason Daniel Sommer left that school never to return.

Also, rationalism and theological liberalism had begun to be preached among the progressive camp, including the denial of Bible miracles, inspiration, etc.

In 1878, Julius Wellhausen published a book denying Mosaic authorship of the Pentateuch. It was not long until such "higher criticism" took hold in the progressive camp. In 1886 George W. Longan gave a lecture for the Missouri Christian Lectureship in which he doubted the logical soundness of Paul's use of allegory in Galatians 3. In 1889, in St. Louis, R.C. Cave preached that the Old Testament fathers were truly ignorant of the character of God. In 1893 the Disciples' Divinity House was opened in Chicago and Herbert L. Willett was assigned to the Semitic Department. Willett was a notorious liberal theologian who denied Daniel's authorship of the Book of Daniel. Such notions simply could not be tolerated by the conservative brethren.

Another doctrine of the progressive movement was fellowship with the pious un-immersed. It became a popular view to regard a person as a Christian and in full fellowship with the body of Christ on the basis of his personality. If this person were deemed a good person that believed in Christ, that was sufficient to call this one a brother or sister in Christ.

The progressive movement also taught that as long as the spirit of the law was upheld, the letter of the law could be avoided. In other words, as long as you felt right about what you were doing, you were accepted by God, regardless of whether or not you were actually and truthfully obeying His will.

By 1890, J.H. Garrison was also leading the charge into full acceptation of denominationalism. He was so bold as to assert that any opposition to denominationalism was contrary to Christ's prayer for unity.

At least three reasons can be said for the rapid acceptance of the progressive doctrine. One, a sense of indifference pervaded many congregations. Brethren simply did not care even to study these issues for themselves. Secondly, weak preaching led to many problems. The first principles of the gospel were replaced by poorly college-educated men who trusted vain philosophies more than the riches of Christ. In the third place, brethren were not thinking for themselves. "Whatever the preacher said must be right," was their attitude.

The Influence of Editors and Christian Journalism

Benjamin Franklin through the *American Christian Review* wielded a tremendous influence in the churches in the North, especially after the Civil War. He was a very sound, conservative editor who helped to check some of the more liberal ideas emerging in the brotherhood at that time. Because he was true to the restoration plea of speaking where the Bible speaks, he was regarded by some as being old fashioned and out of step with the times. You can find many of his articles and sermons reprinted in the *Gospel Preacher* vols. 1 & 2 and in a little book currently out of print titled, *Book of Gems*.

 **John F. Rowe** followed Benjamin Franklin as editor of the ACR. Rowe began with the Review in 1867 and remained until the close of 1886, the last eight years serving as editor.

In 1865 Moses E. Lard said that division was impossible. How wrong he was! During these crucial years it seemed quite obvious that division was not only possible but probable.

Several people, doctrines, and instances contributed to the division. Isaac Errett continued promoting his progressive views in the *Christian Standard* while John F. Rowe opposed him in the *American Christian Review.* Rowe took over this editorship after the death of Benjamin Franklin (1878), and in many ways had a difficult time living up to the standards set by Franklin.

Rowe was oftentimes inconsistent. For example, he believed a small organ could be used, but not a large one. He favored the societies but not the instrument. For a few years Rowe seemed afraid to say what needed to be said about the division being perpetrated by the progressives. When he was pushed, he went on the defensive while forsaking the offensive.

In the northern states, Errett and Rowe were playing a critical game of chess with their papers. Rowe reported on the doctrines being taught among the progressives and Errett accused him of causing division. Errett was quick to play on the sympathy of his readers, as if he was being victimized by the "legalistic" brethren. Errett believed that the majority should rule on the issues of the organ and society and anyone who opposed the majority was guilty of causing division. He did not seem to care about the opinions of the older brethren who had built the congregations which were now being taken from them.

Moses E. Lard (1818-1880) and J.W. McGarvey first worked together on *Lard's Quarterly*. This paper is regarded by many to be one of the finest pieces of Christian journalism to come out of the Restoration Movement. Sadly it ran for only five years (1863-1868) and was discontinued (like many good works) for a lack of funds and support. It appears the brethren at that time did not know what they had, preferring weekly and monthly papers over this quarterly publication. McGarvey and Lard next worked together on the *Apostolic Times*. Along with three other Kentucky preachers, these men used this paper in the 1870's to make a strong stand against the instrument of music in worship.

Isaac Errett and the *Christian Standard* was probably the most influential voice for liberalism in the church of that period. The first issue appeared on April 7, 1866. Errett (1820-1888) had worked with Campbell on the *Harbinger* since 1861 and decided to begin this paper to offset the

influence of Franklin and the *Review* in the northern states. The *Standard* was the only weekly paper to support missionary societies after the war and later was a proponent of instrumental music in worship. Errett was also the first preacher in the church to assume the title, "Reverend." While this title did not catch on, many "progressive" Christian Church preachers who followed Errett used the title, "Pastor." The *Christian Standard* remains the oldest paper and publishing house among the Christian Church.

David Lipscomb continued to use the *Gospel Advocate* to promote the conservative viewpoint in the South. However, its readership was not yet the extent of the *Christian Standard*. Neither was it circulated heavily in the North where the *Standard* remained the prominent paper. We have to understand that during these years most people received their information by and were thus heavily influenced from what they read. He who controlled the readership controlled the mindset for that area.

The *Gospel Advocate* had no shortage of men willing to lay the axe to the root of the problem. This group was headed by David Lipscomb (1831-1917), but he had a little help from his friends.

E.G. Sewell (1830-1924) was Lipscomb's right hand at the *Gospel Advocate*. H. Leo Boles said of Sewell: "Few men who have labored in Tennessee baptized more people than Brother Sewell. Brother Sewell stood with Brother Lipscomb in contending for the faith and simple order of New Testament work and worship. With the exception of Brother Lipscomb, possibly Brother Sewell did more to encourage the churches in the South to remain faithful to the New Testament than any other man. He was kind and gentle in his manner and pleasing in his style of writing and speaking, but he was as sturdy as the oak in standing for the New Testament order of things." *Biographical Sketches of Gospel Preachers*, p.241

Also, **F.D. Srygley** (1856-1900) proved to be a very popular and forceful "front page" columnist for the paper. F.D. Srygley was one of T.B. Larimore's students at Mars Hill in Florence, Alabama. He did not live to be an old man, but left behind some valuable writings especially concerning brother Larimore.

His brother **F.B. Srygley** (1859-1940) was also a powerful writer for the *Gospel Advocate*. He remained on the staff of this paper through a number of editors until his death in 1940. He was very much loved and respected by all. His biography has recently been published titled, *The Warrior from Rock Creek.*

Srygley's book titled *The New Testament Church* is a collection of articles on this subject published in the Gospel Advocate. The style of these articles is clear and forceful; their logic is sound; and the conclusions produced are problematic to any proponent of sectarianism.

E.A. Elam (1855-1929) was a powerful preacher who also wrote for the *Advocate*, and later produced some of the finest annual lesson commentaries ever written, titled "Elam's Notes." It was Elam's gospel meeting in Henderson, Tennessee that proved to be the beginning of the downfall of the pro-instrument group in that town.

J.C. McQuiddy (1858-1924) was the office editor and business manager for the *Gospel Advocate*. The following is taken from H. Leo Boles' *Biographical Sketches of Gospel Preachers*:

"In 1879, F. G. Allen established, in Louisville, Ky., a paper known as *The Old Path Guide*. This paper was the first in magazine form and appeared monthly. The paper grew in influence and circulation. Brother McQuiddy became editorially connected with it in 1883. He traveled extensively in Middle Tennessee and South Kentucky in the interest of the paper. The paper increased rapidly in circulation through his efforts, and it seems that Brother McQuiddy had found his field of activity.

Brother McQuiddy became office editor and business manager of the *Gospel Advocate* in 1885, and moved to Nashville, Tenn. He was twenty-seven years old when he began work with the *Advocate*. Brethren Lipscomb and Sewell made announcement in the first issue of the *Advocate* published in 1885 that arrangements had been completed for Brother McQuiddy to begin work at once...It was largely through Brother McQuiddy's management that the *Gospel Advocate* wielded such a powerful influence in the South."

During this time **M.C. Kurfees** (1856-1931) was very influential in Kentucky. His book on instrumental music in worship shows that by the time of the New Testament onward, the meaning of psallo meant "to sing" exclusively. From H. Leo Boles, *Biographical Sketches of Gospel Preachers*:

"Brother Kurfees was a ready writer and wielded a trenchant pen in written discussions. For many years he was a contributor to the *Gospel Advocate*, and finally became one of the editors of the Advocate in 1908 and continued until 1924—sixteen years.

Brother Kurfees was a cultured, refined, Christian gentleman. He had high regard for honor and would not stoop to anything low or mean. He was a type of Christian manhood that adorns the doctrine of our Lord. His good wife preceded him in death by fifteen years. Brother Kurfees left no children. He will be missed, but we rejoice in the victory which he has won."

James A. Harding (1848-1922) was a great preacher, debater, educator, and also writer for the *Advocate*. He was the first superintendent of the Nashville Bible School (c.1891).

He left there to begin a similar school in Bowling Green, Kentucky. Harding University in Searcy, Arkansas is named for him. Brother Harding was a man dedicated to the New Testament. His biography is titled *The Eyes of Jehovah*, and  was authored by Lloyd Cline Sears. It is a wonderful resource into the life of this good man.

Concerning the "progressive" agenda facing the church in the latter half of the 19th century, James A. Harding wrote:

> "There are many who we are told to 'mark' and 'avoid'; men from whom we are to 'withdraw' ourselves; men who trouble the churches of God by forcing upon them untaught questions; who gratify their own tastes by forcing organs and other such things into the worship, thereby driving numbers of the oldest and best members out. From such let us turn away."

He believed that had this been done sooner many congregations could have been spared. In 1884 Harding observed, "It is an undeniable fact that there are two wings to this reformation and that they are drifting apart."

Eventually Harding's admonition would prevail among conservative brethren. Rather than stay at a place where they felt they could not worship in good conscience, new congregations were started. New schools, such as the Nashville Bible School, helped to counteract the progressive doctrine prevailing in other schools.

Texas Preachers from This Period

Austin McGary (1846-1928) was a fearless gospel preacher. He was a Confederate veteran from Texas who for a time was a "old west" Texas sheriff. He once disarmed and arrested John Wesley

Hardin (a man who killed 27 men). One of the things that lead him to Christ was a critical study of the Campbell-Owen Debate.

McGary was a bitter enemy of the Ku Klux Klan. Once he was preaching in Willis, Texas and was warned to leave town or be killed. McGary responded by sending an old black man to every street corner in that town to shout to the community that on a certain Sunday McGary  would be preaching on the Klan. During this lesson he told how the Klan had taken an old preacher from his home during the night and severely beat him. He told them his door was unlocked at all times, to come any time they wanted, but to bring a wheel-barrel to haul their boys off. He said, "I have a gun and some of you know that I am handy with it." The KKK never bothered Austin McGary again.

McGary is possibly best remembered for being the founder and editor of the *Firm Foundation* in 1884. He began the paper to address the matter of fellowship with others who had not been baptized for the remission of sins. McGary believed such persons needed to be baptized again for the remission of sins. Lipscomb and Harding believed baptism must only be because of faith in Christ, and that a person did not need to know all of the blessings to be received at baptism in order for their baptism to be acceptable to God.

McGary had help from Elijah Hansborough and J.W. Jackson in the early days of this paper. **J.W. Jackson** (1840-1901) was a gospel preacher who was also a Confederate veteran. He had fought at Chancellorsville and Gettysburg. He became a gifted preacher and writer, often using his Civil War experiences to illustrate spiritual truths.

J.D. Tant (1861-1941) was also coming into his prime during this period. J.D. Tant preached all over the nation. Gospel preachers were few and far between. He was in great demand, ordinarily receiving more than 200 invitations per year for gospel meetings. His record was 269 invitations in a single year.

In addition to writing for the *Firm Foundation*, brother Tant also edited the "Texas Department" for the *Gospel Advocate*. His son, Yater, wrote his biography titled, *J.D. Tant: Texas Preacher.*

Joe S. Warlick (1866-1941) was an up and coming gospel preacher during this period. He would debate 399 times over the course of his life. He was an elder at the Pearl and Bryan congregation in Dallas where L.S. White was the local preacher for a while. Bill Lockwood has writ-  ten a biography about his early life (1865-1901), titled, *Events in the Life of Joe S. Warlick.*

L.S. White (1867-1949) was a very effective local preacher in Tennessee and Texas during this period. He was also an effective debater and evangelistic preacher. His best remembered debate came with Charles Taze Russell, the founder of the Jehovah's Witness sect.

The Cause of Division

L.F. Bittle, in the *American Christian Review*, represented **the conservative viewpoint** when he said, "Elijah was not to blame for the drought and famine that for three years or more cursed the land of Samaria. He was not the troubler of Israel as Ahab said. It was the wicked king himself that by departing from the way of the Lord, and bringing in the religious devices of his idolatrous neighbors, had incurred the displeasure of the Almighty, and the prophet was but the instrument of divine vengeance…So it is now…The men who left the New Testament plan of evangelizing, and organized sectarian societies to usurp the authority of Christ by creating offices and delegating powers in spite of brotherly admonition and scriptural argument, persist in their wild schemes, are responsible for all the strife that their plans have enkindled."

W.K. Homan, in the *Christian Courier*, represented **the progressive viewpoint** when he said, "One who admits that the New Testament is silent as to the use of the organ as an aid to the worship of God in song, and yet refuses Christian recognition and fellowship to Christians who exercise the liberty that God has left for them to use such aid, is guilty of flagrant sectarianism in attempting to make a law for God's people where God has made none, and is a divider of the Body of Christ…."

On August 18, 1889, 6,000 members of the church gather in Shelby County, Illinois, for the Sand Creek Meeting. From this meeting the *Sand Creek Address and Declaration* was issued recommending that brethren withdraw fellowship from those using the instrument. Three years later the brethren recommended that churches should put a clause in their property deed declaring that no instrument of music or other innovations should be used on the premises. For writing this document, these brethren, and Daniel Sommer especially, were accused by the *Standard* of abandoning apostolic ground.

 **Daniel Sommer** (1850-1940) was a very conservative preacher during this period. He was burned by the liberalism he found while a student at Bethany College. Perhaps this caused him to take extremes when they were unnecessary. Nev-

ertheless, Sommer was a straightforward, very conservative, light-ning rod of controversy.

By the mid 1890's the conservative position was made clear: either abandon the organ, or fellowship can no longer exist. The cause of this division remains a point of controversy between Christian churches and churches of Christ today. Basically, these views haven't changed.

Timeline of Events 1851-1870

- **April 27, 1851:** Aylette Raines notes in his diary that a brother Saunders wishes to introduce a melodeon in the church services. This is the first mention of such in the Restoration Movement.

- **June 1, 1851:** Thomas Campbell preaches his last sermon at the Bethany church. His text is Matthew 22:37-40.

- **October 1851:** Alexander Campbell writes in the *Harbinger* that instrumental music in worship would be "like a cowbell in a concert."

- **1853: The church is estimated to have a membership of 225,000; 2,700 churches, and 2,250 preachers.**

- **January 4, 1854:** Thomas Campbell dies at Bethany.

- **March 14, 1854:** Jacob Creath, Sr. dies. Henry Clay had called him the finest natural orator he had ever heard.

- **1855:** Northwestern Christian University (now Butler University) opens in Indianapolis.

- **July, 1855:** Tolbert Fanning begins the *Gospel Advocate* from Nashville.

- **January 1, 1856:** Benjamin Franklin begins the *American Christian Review* in Cincinnati.

- **1859:** The Christian Missionary Society is organized in Indianapolis by abolitionists.

- **1860: 225,000 members in 2,070 congregations. The church is seventh overall in size in the nation, but first in rate of growth.**

- **1860:** The church at Midway, Kentucky introduces mechanical instruments into its worship services.

- **April 23, 1861:** Walter Scott dies at Mayslick, Kentucky.

- **September 1863:** Moses E. Lard begins *Lard's Quarterly*.

- ➤ **1865:** The College of the Bible was organized as part of Kentucky University in Lexington, Kentucky.

- ➤ **December 1865**: Alexander Campbell preached his last sermon in the Bethany College chapel.

- ➤ **1866: The national membership of the church is estimated between 400,000 and 600,000.**

- ➤ **1866**: Franklin College closes.

- ➤ **March 4, 1866**: Alexander Campbell dies at his home.

- ➤ **April 7, 1866**: The *Christian Standard* begins publication.

- ➤ **1867:** Benj. Franklin writes that not 10 congregations are using the instrument of music.

- ➤ **Feb. 8, 1868**: Raccoon John Smith preaches his final sermon in Mexico, Missouri. On **Feb. 28,** he dies at the home of his daughter in Mexico, Missouri.

- ➤ **1868:** Buffalo Institute is chartered (it later becomes Milligan College).

- ➤ **1868:** *Lard's Quarterly* ceases publication dues to lack of support.

- ➤ **1869**: The American Christian Missionary Society is changed to the General Christian Missionary Society.

- ➤ **April 15, 1869**: The *Apostolic Times* begins publication in Lexington, Kentucky.

- ➤ **1870: National census shows churches of Christ to be fifth in size, with 350,000 members in 2,822 congregations.**

- ➤ **Jan. 1, 1871** – T.B. Larimore opens Mars Hill Academy in Florence, Alabama.

- ➤ **Sept. – Dec. 1873** – Add-Ran College is chartered in Thorp Springs, TX. This school would later move to Fort Worth and become Texas Christian University.

➤ **May 3, 1874** – Tolbert Fanning dies at his home at Franklin College due to injuries suffered from one of his prize bulls.

➤ **1875 – The church is estimated to have 400,000 members in America.**

➤ **Fall 1875** – The College of the Bible separates from Kentucky University, but fails in 1878. It is now called Lexington Theological Seminary and is under the control of the Disciples of Christ.

➤ **Oct. 20, 1878** – Benjamin Franklin preaches his final sermon. He dies two days later.

➤ **Jan. 1, 1879** – F.G. Allen begins publishing the *Old Path Guide.*

➤ **June 8, 1880** – James A. Garfield is nominated as the Republican candidate for President at the Republican Convention in Chicago.

➤ **Nov. 2, 1880** – James A. Garfield is elected President. He is inaugurated March 4, 1881.

➤ **July 2, 1881** – Garfield is shot in the Washington train station by a disgruntled job-seeker named Charles J. Guiteau. He dies **Sept. 19, 1881**.

➤ **Sept. 20, 1881** – Drake University is founded in Des Moines, Iowa.

➤ **July 2, 1882** – The cornerstone is laid for the Garfield Memorial Church in Washington D.C. It is a subject of controversy, as brethren discuss whether or not it is scriptural to name such things as church buildings or congregations after other brethren.

- ➤ **1883** – Daniel Sommer and B.F. Little begin publishing the *Octograph* (named after the supposed eight writers of the New Testament).

- ➤ **Summer – Fall 1883** – John F. Rowe writes what may have been his best series of articles in the *American Christian Review* titled: "Lift Up a Standard for the People." Isaac Errett takes it as a threat and blames Rowe and others for causing division in the brotherhood.

- ➤ **January 20, 1884** – Garfield Memorial Church is dedicated.

- ➤ **June 1884** – The question of re-baptism is discussed between Austin McGary and David Lipscomb. McGary held that a person needed to be re-baptized who was not originally baptized for the remission of sins. Lipscomb believed that it was sufficient for a person to be baptized knowing only that their baptism was an act of obedience to God. He believed the blessings bestowed at baptism could be learned later.

- ➤ **September 1884** – The *Firm Foundation* begins in Austin, Texas.

- ➤ **1885** – The *Old Path Guide* unites with the *Apostolic Times* to form the *Apostolic Guide*.

- ➤ **1885** – J.C. McQuiddy moves to Nashville to work with the *Gospel Advocate* as office editor and business manager.

- ➤ **August 4, 1885** – The Masonic Male and Female Institute is incorporated as West Tennessee Christian College at Henderson, Tennessee.

- ➤ **December 23, 1886** – Daniel Sommer buys the *American Christian Review*. He would merge it with the *Octograph* and call it the *Octographic Review*.

➢ **1887** – Larimore closes Mars Hill College to conduct gospel meetings fulltime. By 1888, he has 500 calls for meetings.

➢ **May 27 – June 13, 1889** – The "Nashville Debate" is conducted between James A. Harding and J.B. Moody (Baptist). It lasts sixteen nights. Harding follows this debate with a tent meeting on Foster Street in which at least 114 were baptized. (Another source says 117 baptisms.)

➢ **Fall 1889** – A.G. Freed and David H. Nelms open Southern Tennessee Normal College at Essary Springs, TN.

➢ **November 1, 1889** – F.D. Srygley joins the *Gospel Advocate*. The years from 1890-1900 are considered by many as the golden years of the *Advocate*.

➢ **Dec. 1889** – R.C. Cave introduces rationalism in the Central Church at St. Louis. He denies the virgin birth, bodily resurrection, etc.

➢ **1890** – J.H. Garrison publishes articles teaching rationalism.

➢ **1890** – T.B. Larimore conducts a two-month meeting at the Pearl and Bryan Street Congregation in Dallas, TX with 73 additions.

➢ **1890** – Lipscomb and McGary have another round of editorial debates on the subject of re-baptism.

➢ **April 16, 1891** – J.H. Garrison rejects the principles of plurality of elders and advocates the idea of "one real pastor" to oversee the flock.

➢ **April 19 – May 26, 1891** – James A. Harding conducts a tent meeting in Pensacola, Florida with 62 additions. The church grows immediately from 12 to 74.

➢ **October 5, 1891** – Lipscomb and Harding begin the Nashville Bible School.

- **1893** – McGarvey begins a column in the *Christian Standard* titled "Biblical Criticism" to counteract the rationalism being taught by Harrison and others.

- **Fall 1893** – An organ is used at Add-Ran College. This causes division between J.A. Clark and his two sons Addison and Randolph who refused to silence the instrument.

- **January 3 – June 7, 1894** – T.B. Larimore conducts his longest meeting (five months and four days) at Sherman, TX. He preaches 333 sermons and 254 persons were added to the church.

- **February 3, 1894** – A.G. Freed arrives in Henderson, TN to become president of West Tennessee Christian College.

- **1894** – The Disciples Divinity House is established at the University of Chicago with a notorious liberal in Herbert L. Willett serving as Dean.

- **January 3 – April 17, 1895** – Larimore holds a meeting in Los Angeles, CA lasting three months and fourteen days. 120 persons are baptized.

- **Fall 1895** – Add-Ran Christian University moves to Waco, TX, bringing with it the progressive faculty members.

- **Summer 1896** – The Nashville Bible School has completed five years. Its students have converted 3,400 persons and started 28 congregations.

- **1897** – West Tennessee Christian College is changed to Georgie Robertson Christian College upon the donation of $5,000 by her father J.F. Robertson.

- **December 7, 1897** – N.B. Hardeman joins Freed on the faculty of Georgie Robertson.

- **1900** – McGary resigns from the *Firm Foundation.*

➢ **1900** – The Disciples are operating 35 major institutions of higher learning, enrolling 8,000 students, with property worth over $6,000,000.

➢ **1900 – The church has an estimated 1,120,000 members in America.**

Chapter Six

Two Bodies Emerge

1901-1920

By 1900 the church seemed to be at a standstill. Perhaps years of controversy and brotherhood strife were taking their toll. E.G. Sewell observed in the *Gospel Advocate* that churches were not as active as they once were and they were having fewer additions.

That two bodies now existed was obvious. In 1901, A.I. Myhr (a Christian Church preacher and missionary society advocate) issued the fourth edition of the *Year Book* giving only the statistics for the Christian Church.

S.N.D. North was the Director of the Federal Bureau of Census in 1906. He had noticed some overlapping between Christian Church and church of Christ preachers and was curious as to the reason. He wrote to David Lipscomb asking why this was the case on June 17, 1907. Lipscomb informed him that there had been a separation between the two groups, based upon the decision of many to abandon the original intent of restoring New Testament Christianity.

The significance of the 1906 census is that it marked the first official government record of the division between the two groups. However, this was a mere formality. The division had been settled in the minds of brethren for some time by the time of the census.

According to the census of 1906, the combined number of the two groups was 1,142,359 members in 10,942 congregations. Of this number, 982,701 members in 8,293 churches called themselves the Christian Church or Disciples, while 159,685 members in 2,649 congregations were known as the churches of Christ.

The numbers reported for the churches of Christ may have been lower than they actually were. Yet, over the next ten years these numbers doubled. While it could be that the reported numbers in 1906 were on the low side, it could also be that the church simply grew wonderfully at a rate of 99%.

If this is the case, God added approximately 158,279 members to His church during this time to bring the total to 317,937 by 1916. 2,921 congregations were reportedly established during this span which raised the total to 5,570 – a growth rate of 110%.

Growth continued over the next ten years at an estimated rate of 36% in membership and 11% in congregational growth. By 1926 there was an estimated 433,714 members and 6,226 congregations. 115,777 souls were added to the body of Christ during these ten years!

Overall, from 1906 census to the1926 census, the churches of Christ grew by an estimated 274,056 members and 3,577 congregations. The increase of membership was 171% and 135% for congregations. This period marks the most phenomenal period of growth by percentage for the churches of Christ in the Twentieth Century. The church outgrew the nation, even as the nation grew very well (38% from 1906-1926).

On the other hand, the Christian Church/Disciples movement continued to encounter problems. In 1902, they decided to join Protestant churches in the "Federation of Churches and Church Workers." By so doing, these men were simply stating their desire to be one of the denominations. The plea to come out of denominationalism had been lost to them.

In 1909, a Centennial Convention was held by the Disciples in Pittsburg, PA. During this affair, Samuel Hardin (grandson of Barton W. Stone) attacked the old-time beliefs of the brethren, repudiated the Virgin Birth, and stated that baptism should be dispensed with and all denominations should be accepted without it. It is said that the chairman could scarcely quiet the crowd of protestors.

By 1912, at the International Convention of Disciples of Christ which met in Louisville, KY, the Disciples' leaders decided to establish a delegated central organization to manage and control their denomination.

Clearly lines were being drawn among the progressive camp of the Christian Church/Disciples. This division would also unfold in the College of the Bible. By 1917, Hall L. Calhoun charged that "destructive criticism" was being taught in the school. While the school denied such, eventually the truth came out, and this was indeed the case. By 1924 a new college was established in Cincinnati and was known as the Cincinnati Bible Seminary. Hall L. Calhoun later withdrew from the Christian Church to work with churches of Christ.

What lesson can we learn from this period of history? On one hand we can learn of the power found in a resolve to overcome. The churches of Christ became busy, evangelistic, and effective. They showed a "never give up" attitude. Where would the churches of Christ be today without this outstanding period of our history?

On the other hand, the Christian Church/Disciples movement continued to suffer from internal conflict and doctrinal differences. Truthfully, the most radical liberals were being the more consistent according to their "spirit of the letter" philosophy.

New Leaders Emerge

The church said "goodbye" to men like J.W. McGarvey, David Lipscomb, and James A. Harding during this period, but was also introduced to a few new leaders. Basically, the old guard of the *Gospel Advocate* was passing away and a new guard was emerging. You will note, as it has been the case thus far in our study, that whenever one generation passes, another of equal talent and ability is there to receive the "torch" from their brethren.

A.G. Freed (1863-1931) was coming into his own as an educator and preacher during this period. (For more information, read Ancil Jenkins' biography of A.G. Freed. Also, you might enjoy his *Sermons, Chapel Talks, and Debates*.)

Arvy Glenn Freed was born at Saltillo, Indiana in August 3, 1863. He attended local public schools and then Valparaiso University, Valparaiso, Indiana, graduating there in 1889. After graduation he came south and began a teaching, preaching, and debating career at Essary Springs, Tennessee in the fall of 1889.

Essary Springs, where he started his work in Christian Education in the South is on Big Hatchie River in the southeast corner of Hardeman County. Southern Tennessee Normal College, as the school there was named, began in 1889 with Freed as President and continued until 1895. He built it to an enrollment of about 450 students.

In 1895 the board of trustees of West Tennessee Christian College, a school in Henderson, Tennessee that had been in operation for some years, offered to unite the two schools and Freed accepted. He did so under the provision that the trustees would grant him a lease of ten years to run the school. Two years later, in 1897, a new brick administration building was erected and the name of the school was changed to Georgie Robertson Christian College. A period of great growth followed and Brother Freed asserted in 1901 that it was "the largest and best equipped normal school south of the Ohio River."

Due to dissension in the faculty of G.R.C. College, Brother Freed resigned and went to Denton, Texas at the end of his lease in 1905. He became President of Southwestern Christian College and remained there until 1908. He returned to Henderson on that date to become co-founder with N. B. Hardeman of National Teachers

Normal and Business College. He was President and Hardeman Vice-President most of the period from 1908 until 1923. In 1923 he sold his interest in Freed-Hardeman College, (the name of the school having been changed in 1919), and moved to Nashville, Tennessee to become Vice-President of David Lipscomb College, where he remained until his death in 1931. (Adapted from C.P. Roland, *The Minister's Monthly*, January, 1966).

N.B. Hardeman (1874-1965) began his career as an educator in the rural schools of West Tennessee. He was a member of the faculty of Georgie Robertson Christian College for eight years, 1897-1905. In 1908, he and A. G. Freed established the National Teachers' Normal and Business College. It was renamed Freed-Hardeman College in 1919. Hardeman served as Vice President from 1908 to 1920. He served as co-president with Hall L. Calhoun from 1925-1926. He then served as president from 1926-1950.

During almost 60 years as a teacher, perhaps more than 20,000 students sat at Hardeman's feet and studied the Bible and related subjects. He never accepted an appointment as a local minister, but he delivered thousands of sermons, seven volumes of which have been published.

Freed-Hardeman College came into existence because of N. B. Hardeman and A.G. Freed. Their dreams, ideals, and sacrifices brought it into being and these same things have kept it serving a worthwhile purpose to today. (Adapted from *In Memoriam*, by Gussie Lambert)

L.L. Brigance (1879-1950) began preaching in 1902 and continued active until a few months before his death. In the early 1930's, he developed diabetes. Though handicapped by it, he did not al-low it to stop him either from his teaching or his preaching.

For many years, Brigance instructed young preachers in Bible, Church History, and other subjects at Freed-Hardeman College.

His little book of sermon outlines titled *Brigance's Outlines* should be in every gospel preacher's library.

From the plaque which hangs beneath the picture of Brigance in the auditorium at Freed-Hardeman College, W.C. Hall, one of his co-laborers, penned the following words: "It will not be an under-estimate to say that he contacted at least 10,000 students and made them appreciate the principles of the New Testament as no other could have done. He is held in the very highest esteem by all who knew him."

R.L. Whiteside (1869-1951) was born in Hickman County, Tennessee. He attended the Nashville Bible School and sat at the feet of Lip-scomb and Harding. He moved to Abilene, Texas in 1908 to preach for the church there and to teach in the Childers Classical Institute which would  later become Abilene Christian University. The next year when Darden, the president of the school, returned to public schools, Whiteside was chosen to serve as president. During the Whiteside presidency, enrollment grew modestly, and with the help of his small preaching income, and the fact that his wife kept boarders, he was able to pay his teachers, and keep the school going.

During Whiteside's administration, the school sponsored a Special Bible Study Week during the first week of January 1910 and again in 1911. These weeks were the forerunners of the lectureship which began in 1918. Whiteside was elected by the board for a third year but later resigned because West Texas was suffering the effects of a drought that was draining the country of money. He stayed on to teach at the school but in 1914 his association with it came to a close because of poor health.

In 1931 he became a staff writer for the *Gospel Advocate* and produced a weekly article under the heading of "Doctrinal Discourse." His daughter, Inys, compiled many of his articles in the book, *Doctrinal Discourses* in 1955. Perhaps his greatest work of writing was done in his *New Commentary On Paul's Letter to The Saints At Rome.* The first edition of this book was presented to the brotherhood in 1945 and was very favorably received. In 1956, his daughter published the book, *The Kingdom of Promise and Prophecy,* which was a compilation of articles he had written for various publications. The book *Reflections* was published by Inys in 1965 and is a systematic arrangement of articles from the Question and Answer department of the *Gospel Advocate* while he served as Queries Editor for that paper. Inys also published a series of books beginning in 1974 entitled *Bible Studies,* which is also a compilation of Whiteside's writings. When one looks at the prodigious amount of writing he did, one can only wonder how he found the time to do so much effective work.

C.R. Nichol (1876-1961), born in Readyville, TN, is perhaps best remembered for his fine writings. Gussie Lambert notes, "He wrote twenty one books during his lifetime. His booklet, "Nichol's Pocket Bible Encyclopedia," has sold well over a million copies and his publication, "Sound Doctrine," has been reprinted by request in Japanese, German, and Spanish languages. "Sound Doctrine," Volumes 1, 2, 3, and 4 are used as textbooks for graduate class work in all Christian colleges in the United States and can be found in most all colleges and university libraries regardless of denomination." "Sound Doctrine" was also the title of his column in the *Gospel Advocate.*

While, Nichol was an excellent writer and preacher, perhaps he was even more effective as a debater. From a very young age he proved himself to be worthy of defending the faith and confounded false teachers of every sect.

His biography, written by Maude Jones Underwood, is titled *A Preacher of Righteousness*.

 **Foy E. Wallace, Sr.** (1871-1949) was born June 2, 1871, at Decatur, Texas. He was a great gospel preacher and defender of the ancient gospel. He was known by many as the "Dean of Texas Ministers" when he died (*Gospel Guardian*, December 1, 1949).

Brother Wallace began preaching at the age of twenty-one in the rural communities of East Texas. He also did mission work in the Indian Territory in the early 1890s. Of this period, Gussie Lambert wrote:

"While there, near what became Mansville, Oklahoma, he made friends with the miners by greeting them as they entered and returned from the mines. In those early days, religious prejudices were rife and tempers short. Freedom of speech was an ideal not understood or practiced. The strange doctrine of a pure gospel was a new thing not understood or respected. So, some of the men of the community resolved to 'stop that preacher.' The news leaked out that they intended to ride the preacher out of town on a rail. The miners got together and stood watch at the windows. When the men arose from the audience, with "throw the preacher out," the miners replied, 'sit down and let the man speak,' and they backed up their authority with drawn pistols. Such was the temperament of the place and times" (Gussie Lambert, *In Memoriam*, pg. 282 ff.).

His daughter, Willie, said that brother Wallace never issued a challenge for a debate, but never refused to defend the truth when challenged. She told of one such debate which occurred in 1910, while brother Wallace lived in Sherman, Texas. He went to Oklahoma to meet a Baptist minister named Cagle in debate. When the debate was over, he sent a telegram home informing the family that he would remain for another week to hold a meeting. Later, during the week, he heard someone remark that Cagle was bragging about how he whipped him in the debate. Wallace remarked, "I baptized his moderator, his son-in-law, two of his elders, and many of his members, 19 in all. If he calls that victory, I am glad to concede it." (Willie Wallace Speck, "I Remember My *Dad.*" *Gospel Advocate*, March 23, 1978).

On February 2, 1890, he married Martha Ann Higgins. To this union, nine children were born. On September 13, 1913, Martha Ann "Mattie" died after a prolonged illness.

On October 8, 1914, he married Jewell Jacobs. Two sons, Paul and Tom, were born to this union. "Mother Jewell" as she was known was very much beloved by the entire family. Both Martha Ann and Jewell were laid to rest beside the grave of brother Wallace. Four of his sons became gospel preachers: Cled, Foy E., Jr., Paul, and Tom.

Wallace died November 21, 1949, at Tyler. He is buried in the cemetery in Georgetown, Texas.

 **H. Leo Boles** (1874-1946) succeeded Lipscomb as the great leader of the church in Middle Tennessee. He served as president of the Nashville Bible School which was changed to David Lipscomb College after brother Lipscomb's death. And he also wrote for and edited the *Gospel Advocate* for a while. Brother Boles was also one of the best writers from this period. His work

on the Holy Spirit is considered by many to be the finest ever produced on Him. Much more could be said about brother Boles. I recommend that you read his biography titled, "I'll Stand on the Rock." Gussie Lambert said of Boles:

"His greatest work was during the years that he served as teacher and president of David Lipscomb College. He was president from 1913 to 1920 and from 1923 to 1932. As teacher, president, and member of the Board of Trustees, he was associated with the college almost a third of a century. When he began preaching, he went out first to the hard places and preached to small congregations. In 1904, he held six meetings with 153 additions and received for the six meetings, $168.63. In 1905, he held 12 meetings with 170 additions and received $229.15.

"His great ability, sincerity and devotion soon placed him before the largest congregations in the brotherhood. He was a voluminous writer. For almost 40 years, Boles wrote for the *Gospel Advocate* as contributor, editor and staff writer. He wrote commentaries on the gospel of Matthew, the book of Luke, and the book of Acts. He also wrote a book on the Holy Spirit. He engaged in public discussion on various subjects that faced the brotherhood. The Boles-Boll Debate on premillennialism has proved a source of valuable instruction for those confronted with the issue. He also engaged in the Boles-Clubb discussion which contains a great amount of discussion and information on instrumental music in the worship of the church. He also wrote a book on biographical sketches of gospel preachers and set before the brotherhood many great preachers that we had forgotten through the years. The *Gospel Advocate* devoted the entire issue of March 28, 1946, in honor of Henry Leo Boles. Seventy writers expressed their gratitude, love and appreciation for this great brother in Christ."

 **S.H. Hall** (1877-1961) started the Central church of Christ in Los Angeles, and the congregation in Madison, Tennessee. He also established congregations among the Japanese in Los Angeles and many Negro congregations in the deep South. He was directly responsible for establishing more than 100 congregations. Perhaps one of his most successful labors was at the Russell Street Church of Christ in Nashville, Tennessee, where he preached for 28 years.

R.H. Boll (1875-1956) was an outstanding preacher in his youth. Sadly, he is best remembered for his premillennial views and advocacy of this doctrine. He was also a writer and editor of religious journals. In 1901 he became one of the editors of the *Gospel Guide*. From 1909-1915 he was the front page  editor of the *Gospel Advocate*. About that time he purchased the monthly magazine, *Word and Work*, removed it from New Orleans to Louisville, and assumed the work of publishing and editing that paper for many years. Like Jesse B. Ferguson, Boll never reached his full ability and became somewhat of an outcast because of his strange convictions.

The pre-millennial controversy in churches of Christ during the Twentieth Century came in large part because of the teachings of R.H. Boll. He was a talented writer and preacher and was very much respected in the church. He held his greatest influence around the Louisville, KY, area where he preached for many years.

In 1909 he became the front-page editor of the *Gospel Advocate* until 1915 when he was forced to resign because of his speculative teaching on millennial themes. Boll had been studying the works of Charles T. Russell (the founder of the Jehovah's Witnesses) and had become enthralled with the idea of Christ's return and establishment of a 1,000 year reign in Jerusalem. He was told to keep his views private by the men at the *Gospel Advocate*, but Boll considered them to be a matter of faith and refused to do so.

Boll pressed his views in his new paper, *Word and Work*. He also circulated many tracts and books on this theme, hoping to sway brethren into agreement with him. He denounced the men of the *Gospel Advocate* for being sectarian in their mindset, having not allowed him to teach his views in that paper. However, because of his influence some Louisville churches withdrew fellowship from brethren who would not hold to Boll's doctrine.

Boll did not stop at writing. He established Kentucky Bible College for the purpose of training preachers to teach his views. He recruited and sent out a number of foreign missionaries. Most were missionaries of his millennial doctrine.

In 1927 H. Leo Boles took issue with Boll in a written debate. The discussion was carried on the pages of the *Gospel Advocate* and *Word and Work* and was later published in book form. The tide was clearly turning against Boll with great might.

His views were debated and became the subject of many sermons even unto this present day. Foy E. Wallace, Jr. fought this doctrine with great force. It is largely due to the writings of brother Wallace that the doctrine did not gain traction among churches.

 **H.L. Calhoun** (1863-1935) is best remembered as being one of the best educated men of this period. He held degrees from the College of the Bible, Yale, and Harvard. He taught for the College of the Bible, Freed-Hardeman College, and David Lipscomb College.

Calhoun is also remembered for his very popular radio broadcast. Untold thousands of people heard Calhoun preach the gospel over Nashville radio station WLAC. Today, this remains the longest running religious broadcast in America.

E.M. Borden was an outstanding gospel preacher and debater. He debated such men as L.S. Ballard and Ben Bogard. His book, "Life, Incidents, and Sermons of Eli Monroe Borden" gives us the best insight into this man.

Joe Blue (1875-1954) was a great preacher in Arkansas. His name is still revered in that state among faithful brethren. He endured many hardships while preaching. On one occasion a stick of dynamite was placed beneath is podium and  the fuse was lit while he was preaching. Thankfully the fuse went out before it reached him.

When brother Blue moved to the Morriston community near Salem, AR, many denominations existed there and the church of Christ was very small. When he moved from there some fifty years later, only the church of Christ remained and it was very strong and active.

To learn more about Joe Blue and other early Arkansas preachers, the book "Arkansas Angels" by Boyd Morgan is very helpful. Also, Wilson's "Arkansas Christians" is a helpful follow-up.

Black Evangelists

An entire book could and should be devoted to the early black evangelists in the churches of Christ. Such men include **S.W. Womack, Alexander Cleveland Campbell**, and **G.P. Bowser**. However, the best remembered is **Marshall Keeble** (1878-1968). Brother Keeble is probably my personal favorite of all the preachers we have discussed. It is estimated that he baptized 40,000 people in his life. Several biographies and one autobiography have been written about him. You can also find a few of his sermons recorded on the internet.

Marshall Keeble began preaching in Nashville, Tennessee in 1897, preaching at the Jackson Street church of Christ. He established over 200 congregations over the next sixty years of preaching. Sometimes he would baptize over 100 people in a single gospel meeting.

In the 1930s he wrote to the *Gospel Advocate* stating that he had baptized over 15,000 people. Estimates range from between 20,000 and 40,000 people who were baptized by this great gospel preacher.

 He was an evangelist that was influential among both African American and Caucasian people. He preached throughout America and also made numerous trips to Nigeria.

In 1942 he became the first president of the Nashville Christian Institute. The Institute opened its doors in 1940 as a night school for adults. When Keeble became president, it began offering day classes to young people, ultimately developing into a K-12th grade school. He served as president until 1958.

He held many debates in his lifetime. His first debate was with his father, Robert, who had attached himself to a religious group called "Do-Rights." The debate was over foot-washing and The Lord's Supper (The "Do-Rights" used water in the place of grape juice.)

A book was edited and produced by B.C. Goodpasture and the Gospel Advocate in 1931 called, *Biography and Sermons of Mar-*

shall Keeble. He wrote his autobiography, *History of My Life (or) Mule Back To Super Jet With The Gospel*, printed by the *Gospel Advocate* in 1962. In 1968 a biography was released by J.E. Choate and the Gospel Advocate titled, *Roll Jordan Roll.*

Brother Keeble died April 20, 1968. B.C. Goodpasture preached his funeral. Over 3,000 people were in attendance.

Timeline of Events 1901-1920

➤ **1901** – The Nashville Bible School is incorporated. James A. Harding leaves the school to begin a new one in Bowling Green, Kentucky (Potter Bible College). William Anderson follows Harding as head of the Nashville Bible School and serves until his death in 1905. E.A. Elam is also added as a board member this year.

➤ **1901** - A.I. Myhr (a Christian Church preacher and missionary society advocate) issued the fourth edition of the *Year Book* giving only the statistics for the Christian Church.

➤ **October 8, 1901** – Potter Bible College opens with 107 students. This school closed in 1913.

➤ **October 1901** – McGarvey resigns as an elder of the Broadway congregation in Lexington, Kentucky, due to deafness. On Nov. 2, 1902, this congregation introduced the instrument, causing McGarvey to leave and place membership with the Chestnut Street congregation.

➤ **1902** – Disciples decide to join Protestant churches in the "Federation of Churches and Church Workers."

➤ **1903** – Gunter Bible College opens in Gunter, Texas. It closed in 1928.

➤ **January 1903** – E.A. Elam conducts a meeting in Henderson, Tennessee, which leads to the beginning of a non-instrumental congregation in that town.

➤ **1906** – R.H. Boll begins editing *Word and Work*.

➤ **1906 – 1911** – N.L. Clark edits the *Firm Foundation*.

➤ **1906** – The census taken showed the combined number of the two groups (Christian Church and churches of Christ) was

1,142,359 members in 10,942 congregations. Of this number, 982,701 members in 8,293 churches called themselves the Christian Church or Disciples, while 159,685 members in 2,649 congregations were known as the churches of Christ. These numbers were released in 1910.

➢ **1906** - The Childers Classical Institute opened its doors in Abilene, Texas with 25 students enrolled for classes. This is the forerunner to Abilene Christian College (c.1920).

➢ **1907** – Georgie Robertson Christian College closes

➢ **May 21, 1907** – The National Teachers' Normal and Business College was incorporated and construction of the Administration Building began that fall. Classes began in 1908. This is the forerunner to Freed-Hardeman College (c. 1919).

➢ **1909** - A Centennial Convention was held by the Disciples in Pittsburg, Pennsylvania.

➢ **1912** – At the International Convention of Disciples of Christ which met in Louisville, Kentucky, the Disciples' leaders decided to establish a delegated central organization to manage and control their denomination.

➢ **1913** – Potter Bible College closes

➢ **1915** – R.H. Boll is removed from the staff of the *Gospel Advocate* for teaching premillennialism

➢ **1917** – Hall L. Calhoun charged that "destructive criticism" was being taught in the College of the Bible. In 1924 a new college was established in Cincinnati, known as the Cincinnati Bible Seminary, to combat the liberalism being taught in the College of the Bible.

Chapter Seven

Christian Education and Orphan Homes

New Colleges Established

The only colleges which remained with those who desired to adhere faithfully to New Testament Christianity after the split of the 19th century was the Nashville Bible School (now Lipscomb University) and **Burritt College** in Spencer, Tennessee (1848-1939).

In Texas a number of colleges were established but later failed. These include: Lockney Christian College, Gunter Bible College, Clebarro College, and Sabinal College. The 1930's witnessed the closing of Thorp Spring Christian College, Cordell Christian College, and Burritt College.

Potter Bible College

Potter Bible College ran from 1901-1913. The school began when Clinton C. Potter and his wife Mary offered their farm in Bowling Green, KY, for the site for a new school. James A. Harding and his son-in-law J.N. Armstrong agreed to work in founding the school.

Harding, who opposed endowments and fixed salaries, desired that the school be funded by the proceeds from the 140 acre Potter farm. The school never became self-supporting, however, and was forced to close in 1913. The land has since been used to operate Potter's Orphan Home.

Freed-Hardeman College

In August of 1885, West Tennessee Christian College was founded in Henderson, TN. On the first Monday in October, the college opened with J.B. Inman as its president. President Inman died in 1889, and G.A. Lewellen was elected president. Lewellen resigned in 1893, and C.H. Duncan was elected to succeed him.

In 1895, Arvy Glenn Freed, an alumnus of Valparaiso University in Indiana who had become, in 1889, the first president of Southern Tennessee Normal College at Essary Springs, Tennessee, became president of West Tennessee Christian College. The name of the college was changed to Georgie Robertson Christian College in 1897. The name was changed when her father J.F. Robertson donated $5,000 to the school.

In 1902, Ernest C. McDougle became co-president with Freed, and when Freed resigned in 1905, McDougle continued as president until the college closed at the end of the spring term in 1907. During this time, R.P. Meeks was the head of the Bible Department, and very pro-instrument.

In fact, Henderson was known as the one stronghold for the Christian Church in West Tennessee. Men like Freed, L.L. Brigance, and a young man named N.B. Hardeman were all aligned with the Christian Church for a while.

All of this changed in the first decade of the Twentieth Century in large part to the influence of Freed, who had recently come to abandon the instrument. E.A. Elam was asked to come to Henderson and conduct a meeting in which the issue of the instrument was discussed fully in light of the Scriptures. He arrived in January of 1903. His meeting led to one of the finest and widest circulated debates on the subject. The debate took place between J. Carroll Stark of Hamilton, IL and Joe S. Warlick. It was a four day debate which began on November, 24, 1903. Within four years the Christian Church element was all but nonexistent, and Henderson has been a stronghold for churches of Christ ever since.

E.C. McDougle closed Georgie Robertson College in 1907 and refused to sell the property to the church of Christ people who wanted to keep the school going. Thus, on May 21, 1907, the National Teachers' Normal and Business College was incorporated and construction of the Administration Building began that fall.

The new college opened in the fall of 1908 with A.G. Freed as president and N. B. Hardeman, who had studied and taught at Georgie Robertson Christian College, as vice president. The college was renamed for them in 1919. In February of 1990, it became Freed-Hardeman University.

Abilene Christian
(from the A.C.U. website)

"A.B. Barret and Charles Roberson were riding in a buggy near Barret's home in Denison, Texas, on their way to a gospel meeting when Barret first said to Roberson, "Let's build a school in West Texas.""

That was in 1903. In 1905, Barret, a teacher at Southwestern Christian College in Denton, was finally able to make a site survey. The Church of Christ in Abilene was growing solidly, and after Barret preached there in December 1905, members agreed to help support the project. Barret soon moved west and traveled by buggy with his wife and friends to raise more support.

Col. J.W. Childers, a leader in the Abilene church, agreed to sell Barret some land he owned west of town and deducted about $2,000 from the price of the land on the condition that the school would be named in his honor. The Childers Classical Institute opened its doors in the fall of 1906 with 25 students enrolled for classes.

The five acres occupied by the institute included the old Childers mansion, a two-story frame house used as the president's

108

home and girl's dormitory. Boys boarded in private homes approved by the president. An eight-room administration building was constructed on the site for $8,000.

Only the 11 primary and secondary grades were offered that first semester. College courses were not accredited for eight years. By the end of the first school year 85 students were enrolled.

Childers' first years were difficult for everyone, particularly the students. Cold classrooms, crowded living conditions and a water shortage necessitated hard work and ingenuity on the part of everyone. The school went through four presidents during those early years: Barret, H.C. Darden, R.L. Whiteside, and James F. Cox, who served another term as president from 1931-1940.

To complicate matters, Col. Childers hired an attorney to collect on a note he had retained on the land and mansion. The school had to borrow money at 15 percent interest to pay the debt, making it difficult to meet operating expenses.

A good businessman was needed and found in Jesse P. Sewell, who became the president in 1912. Sewell declined the offer of a salaried position as president, opting instead to run the school as though it were a personal business enterprise. Sewell certainly didn't get rich in the deal, but the college benefited from approximately $60,000 donated to the school by the Sewells during his 12-year presidency.

With Sewell's new approach came a new identity for the school. Since its beginning the Institute had been commonly referred to as Abilene Christian or the Christian college in Abilene. When Sewell became president, the school began using the name Abilene Christian College in its catalog and other printed materials.

Lawrence Smith explained that the original deed to the Childers land required that the school be named after the colonel. Childers' heirs threatened to sue if the name were changed. In 1920, the school paid the family $4,000 and formally changed its name to Abilene Christian College.

Sewell's leadership brought the college out of debt. The campus was enlarged by four new brick buildings, an enlarged administration building and six frame structures, and an increased enrollment of about 300 students during his final term. Sewell's reign also resulted in accreditation as a junior college in 1914 and as a senior college in 1919."

Harding College
(from Harding University's website)

"Harding began as a senior college in 1924, when two junior colleges, Arkansas Christian College and Harper College, merged their facilities and assets, adopted the new name of Harding College, and located on the campus of Arkansas Christian in Morrilton, Ark. Harper had been founded in 1915 in Harper, Kan., and Arkansas Christian had been chartered in 1919.

Upon completion of a study begun in May 1978, the board of trustees approved the study's recommended change of Harding to university status, and on Aug. 27, 1979, the name of the institution officially became Harding University.

The college was named in memory of James A. Harding, co-founder and first president of Nashville Bible School (now David Lipscomb University) in Nashville, Tenn. A preacher, teacher and Christian educator, James A. Harding inspired his co-workers and associates with an enthusiasm for Christian education that remains a significant tradition at Harding University.

With the merger J.N. Armstrong, who had served five years as Harper's president, became president of Harding College, and A.S. Croom, president of Arkansas Christian for two years, became vice

110

president for business affairs. In 1934 Harding was moved to its present site in Searcy, Ark., on the campus of a former women's institution, Galloway College.

One of Harding's first graduates, George S. Benson, returned from mission work in China in 1936 to assume the presidency of his alma mater. The vigorous educator quickly directed the College out of deep indebtedness and launched it on a journey to financial stability, national recognition, and academic accreditation. When Dr. Benson retired in 1965, his 29 years of tireless service were more than evident in a multimillion-dollar campus, regional accreditation, a strong faculty, and a continually growing student body. Dr. Benson died in December 1991 and is buried in Searcy."

George Pepperdine College
(excerpts taken from Pepperdine's website)

 **George Pepperdine (1886 - 1962)** was the founder and president of the Western Auto Supply Company which the newlywed alumnus of Parsons Business College in Kansas, at the age of 23, started with an initial investment of five dollars in 1909. In the following decades Mr. Pepperdine rode the wave to phenomenal business success providing quality automotive products and services via a network of hundreds of retail stores to an American nation just beginning its love affair with the automobile.

On September 21, 1937, the new campus of George Pepperdine College hosted 2,000 attendees gathered to witness the opening of the school. Speakers that day included California governor Frank Merriam, Los Angeles mayor Frank L. Shaw, the college's first president Batsell Baxter, and founder George Pepperdine. Among the crowd were the college's first students, 167 young men and women from 22 states and two foreign countries. Mr. Pepperdine clearly stated his intentions for the school on that day: "Our college is dedicated to a twofold objective: First, academic training in the liberal arts ... Secondly, we are especially dedicated to a greater goal—that of building in the student a Christ-like life, a love for the church, and a passion for the souls of mankind."

The campus was located in the Vermont Knolls area of Los Angeles, a few miles south of downtown; formerly it had been a 34-acre estate with an 18-room mansion that had now been converted into the president's residence. Four buildings had quickly risen that year: Baxter Hall, the men's dormitory; Marilyn Hall, the women's residence; an administration building housing classrooms, offices, a library, and an auditorium; and a dining hall. The campus architecture was built in the Streamline Moderne style, and all of the new buildings were painted a light blue which was later marketed in Los Angeles paint stores as "Pepperdine Blue."

In 1937, tuition was low relative to other schools, thanks to Mr. Pepperdine's initial endowment, with room, board, tuition, and fees amounting to $420. Those who today would be called "commuter" students were charged $135 for the year. By contrast, a hamburger and soft drink in the cafeteria cost 20 cents, a breakfast of eggs, hotcakes, and coffee, 30 cents.

The [Batsell] Baxter presidency was short by design, lasting only two years until his resignation in June 1939, but his brief tenure which took advantage of his experience in presiding over two other Christian colleges, David Lipscomb College and Abilene Christian College, was characterized by creating sound academic and administrative foundations and thoughtful traditions. During the college's first year of operation, only seven months after opening, Pepperdine received full accreditation from the Northwest Association, the regional accrediting authority. Baxter and dean Hugh Tiner, who succeeded Baxter as president, recruited a faculty of 22, of whom three held doctorates. And on June 6, 1938, after one year of operation, Pepperdine celebrated its first commencement awarding diplomas to a graduating class of four.

The Charity of A.M. Burton (1879-1966)

 Andrew Mizell Burton founded the Life and Casualty Insurance Company of Tennessee in 1903. He was baptized at the Highland Avenue church of Christ in Nashville in 1910. His growing interest in religion led him to make contributions to more than 1000 churches of Christ throughout the world, and he was instrumental in the establishment and development of Central church of Christ in downtown Nashville.

With little education himself, he became the chief inspiration and support of David Lipscomb College and the Nashville Christian Institute and made personal contributions to numerous educational institutions throughout the nation and the world.

Orphan Homes Established

This was an exciting period for benevolent works in the church. Brethren all over the country began recognizing the need to be more active in the care of the widow and fatherless. (Note: Most of the information appearing in this portion of our study came from the websites associated with these homes.)

Arkansas Christian Home (now Southern Christian Home) and **Potter Orphan Home** were both housed on former college campuses. ACH began on May 8, 1926 on the first campus of Harding College in Morrilton, Arkansas. POH began on the old Potter Bible College campus in Bowling Green, Kentucky.

Belle Haven Orphan's Home was primarily the result of the charity of a Christian woman named Jennie Clark. She had opened

113

her home at Luling, Texas, to orphaned children before World War I. However, a devastating cyclone wrecked her home on April 5, 1918. Determined to persevere, she reached out to people in the community and her brethren and by 1921 she was caring for 53 children! Sadly, however, her home and dream died with her. She was facing failing health and financial misfortune in her later years and without the help and support she needed, the home melted away.

Boles Orphan Home was established near Greenville, Texas, on Thanksgiving Day, 1924. Flavil L. Colley had been approached by Mr. and Mrs. W.F. Boles concerning a tract of land they wished to give to be used for an orphanage. Flavil then went to his father, A.O. Colley, and the church where his father preached, the renowned Pearl and Bryan congregation in Dallas, to see about overseeing the project. This home has been one of the best and most successful through the years. The following is from their website.

The Home began in 1924 on a 436 acre tract of land donated by William Foster Boles and his wife, Mary Barnhart Boles for the care of children. Having been originally established as a home for orphans, it currently has been expanded to serve the needs of troubled youth. Through the love and support of over 300 congregations of churches of Christ (and other interested groups and individuals) the Home has continued to care for more than 20,000 children in its 83 year history.

The Home is a non-profit corporation with an eleven-member Board of Directors. Board members are appointed with the concurrence of the elders of the Skillman Church of Christ in Terrell, Texas.

The **Tipton Orphan Home** was established early in 1921 in Canadian, Texas. The home moved to Tipton, Oklahoma, near the end of 1922.

From the beginning, The Tipton Home trustees were composed of the elders of the Tipton church of Christ. The elders were L. A. Todd, H. N. Seymour, R. E. Chitwood, S. D. Jackson and Sol Tipton. Robert E. Chitwood took on the work of being the superintendent of The Tipton Orphans' Home. By the early summer of 1927, The Tipton Home family had increased to 220. In September of 1927, there were 158 children in the first six grades. Forty-seven children were above the sixth grade level, and they were made a part of the public school system of Tipton. The first six grades went to school at The Tipton Home.

The **Sunny Glen Home** opened March 29, 1936, in Mercedes, Texas. The following is taken from their website.

"Sunny Glen Children's Home began in 1936 by offering residential care to 6 children in a two-story house near La Feria, Texas. During its first year, child placement demand was so great that the home moved to a larger facility in San Juan, Texas, that could house up to 30 children.

In 1945, Sunny Glen purchased an 80 acre tract of land in San Benito, Texas in order to expand its services to more children. Construction began in 1948 and, in 1949, Sunny Glen moved to its present location. Sunny Glen Children's Home now has four cottages capable of comfortably housing 32 children and their houseparents."

Tennessee Orphan Home began in 1909 in Columbia, Tennessee. It is now in the nearby community of Spring Hill. The following is from their website.

"In 1909, Tennessee Orphan Home began in Columbia, Tennessee, to meet the needs of the three Scotten children who were tragically orphaned. In 1935, the Home purchased the campus of

115

the Branham and Hughes Military Academy and moved to Spring Hill, Tennessee.

Since 1909, over ten thousand children have been cared for at the Home. As with many of the old orphanages, the Home was designed as an institutional facility with central dining, central laundry, dormitory living and a small farming operation. The approach to child care was to provide the basic physical needs of children and to offer Christian instruction.

In 1988, the Home increased the number of children served under its direction merging with West Tennessee Children's Home. Continued growth in our service area occurred again in 2000 and 2001 through mergers with Happy Hills Youth Ranch near Ashland City and East Tennessee Christian Services in Knoxville."

The **Shultz-Lewis Children's Home** (from their website) began in 1947 when Elmer and Deborah Lewis donated 500 acres of farmland in Morgan Township just south of Valparaiso, Indiana, for the purpose of providing Christian care for children in need. After the facility was built and a staff was assembled, the first children were provided care in the spring of 1956. Since that time, over fifteen hundred children have been served at Shultz-Lewis.

Chapter Eight

Crucial Years

1921-1940

Let us now study the era that fell between World War I and World War II. The nation surely went through a lot during this era. America experienced two world wars, the roaring twenties, and the Great Depression.

The church also experienced its share of disappointments and triumphs during this period. All in all, however, it was another phenomenal period of growth.

From 1926-1945, the church grew by a reported 166,286 souls – an increase of 38%. 1,774 new congregations are believed to have been established during this period for an increase of 28%.

During the span of 1926-1936, the church's membership reportedly grew from 433,714 to approximately 500,000. The newly added 66,286 souls increased the body by 15%. An estimated 474 congregations were established during this time, bringing the total from 6,226 to 6,700 for an increase of 8%. During this time the nation grew at a rate of 9%.

Growth increased greatly over the next nine years (1936-1945). It was reported that 100,000 souls were added from 1936-1945 increasing the body by 20% to 600,000. It is said that 1,300 congregations were established during this period for an increase of 19%, bringing the total to approximately 8,000. The nation grew at a rate of 7%, while the church grew at a rate of 20%.

Even when the nation's population was not increasing at a rapid rate the church reportedly grew wonderfully. What a wonderful lesson to learn from this period of our history! Truly this is a valuable lesson for small town and rural churches who suppose that, because their town population is not rapidly growing, the church cannot grow.

The gospel can have a powerful effect and souls can be saved regardless of whatever barrier we might suppose. The church can have a bright future in a rapidly growing community or a peaceful small town setting. While one congregation may have three talents as compared to another congregation's one talent, success remains dependent upon faithfulness, not the setting, or rate of growth in a given community.

Leaders from this Era

G.H.P. Showalter (1870-1954) received his education at the Greendale Institute in Virginia, Milligan College in Tennessee, and the University of Texas. He taught school and did evangelistic work in Virginia and West Virginia from 1892 to 1897. Showalter came to Texas in 1897 and was President of Sabinal Christian College where he served for one year. He began preaching at Greendale, Virginia, in 1891, and was an active preacher of the gospel for nearly 63 years.

In 1908, Showalter became the editor and owner of the *Firm Foundation* and he continued in this work until the time of his death. He baptized all six of his children and all of his grandchildren that were old enough to obey the gospel during his life. He conducted the marriage ceremony for all of his children. This is one of the highest compliments that children and grandchildren can pay to their father and grandfather.

G.C. Brewer (1884-1956) began preaching at the age of 16 in Florence, Alabama. He preached in all the States in the Union except the States along the Canadian border.

During his last years, and until almost the moment of death, he was chiefly active in, and found his greatest satisfaction from, editing the *Voice of Freedom*, a paper designed to awaken the people in and out of the church to the threat of Catholicism and Communism, both religiously and politically inclined. It is our conviction that the stature of G.C. Brewer will continue to increase with the passing of the years; and that he will take his place, in the final estimate of history, among the greatest of recent generations.

In addition to his regular local work with a congregation, he usually held about twelve meetings each year. He was a prolific writer and some of his books included: *The Model Church, Brewer's Sermons, Contending For the Faith,* and *Forty Years On The Firing Line.* Brewer wrote an autobiography during the last months of his life. He died June 9, 1956, at Searcy, Arkansas.

 **Batsell Baxter** (1886-1956) is best remembered as an educator, although he was also a fine gospel preacher. He taught school at Thorp Springs Christian College, Abilene Christian College, Cordell Christian College and Harding College. He was president of Abilene Christian College from 1924-32, president of David Lipscomb College, 1932-1934, and again in 1943-1946. He was president of George Pepperdine College, 1937-1939. He became president emeritus and head of the Bible Department at David Lipscomb in 1946. He wrote regularly for the *Gospel Advocate* for 26 years and was a highly respected member of its staff.

He was a man like Moses in his meekness. He was a man of vision, a man who encouraged young men to prepare for places of leadership, and was willing to step down and encourage them in taking the lead. He thoroughly believed in Christian education. After Abilene Christian president Don Morris had received news of Baxter's death, he opened a letter from Baxter expressing appreciation for the wonderful lectureship week in Abilene. The letter contained a check for Abilene College. Truly, a great prince in Israel died on March 4, 1956, when Baxter went to be with his Lord.

Baxter began preaching in 1908 in Nashville, Tennessee. He preached in numerous places, particularly in Corsicana, Texas, and had numerous appointments around the Christian colleges where he taught. He preached the gospel in 21 States.

 **Foy E. Wallace, Jr.,** (1896-1979) was the son of the highly regarded Texas preacher, Foy E. Wallace, Sr. (see pages 92-93). Foy E. Wallace Jr. was from a family of many faithful gospel preachers, including his father, his uncles, his three brothers, and his sons and grandsons. He preached his first sermon at Stephenville, Texas, at the age of 15. His parents moved to Thorp Spring, Texas, where a Christian college had begun in 1910, so that their children would be able to attend. Foy enrolled there in January, 1915.

Wallace married Virgie Brighwell when he was 18. She was 16. They were married for 65 years until Foy's death in 1979. All their children became faithful Christians. When home obligations permitted, after the children were reared, Virgie traveled with Foy to support his preaching in gospel meetings. During one of his meetings, she suffered a stroke. Foy made every effort to aid her rehabilitation. This included going to the Hot Springs, Arkansas, health resort so noted for its therapies. She never recovered fully. In later years she was confined to a wheelchair. Brother Wallace always showed tender care. She kept traveling with him and Foy kept pushing her gently and lovingly in her wheel chair.

In 1923, at age 27, his preaching took him east of the Mississippi River for the first time. His powerful preaching at the Russell Street church of Christ in Nashville attracted overflow audiences. Those who heard him there would never forget the occasion.

In August of 1930 he became the youngest editor in the history of the *Gospel Advocate* at age 34. For the rest of his life, brother Wallace fought to keep premillennialism out of churches of Christ. First, he did so from the pages of the *Gospel Advocate*, then from his own papers: the *Bible Banner*, the original *Gospel Guardian*, and *Torch*. *God's Prophetic Word* is perhaps his most acclaimed book. It is a definitive treatment of the doctrine of premillennialism.

Wallace was also a champion debater. Among his most notable were the two debates in 1933 with Charles M. Neal concerning premillennialism; his debate with Dr. J. Frank Norris in 1934 in Fort Worth, Texas; Dr. E.F. Webber in Oklahoma City, Oklahoma, in 1937; and with Glen V. Tingley in Birmingham, Alabama, in 1938. Each of these debates was on the subject of premillennialism and Baptist doctrine.

He also had several debates on the subject of instrumental music in worship. In 1944, he traveled to California to debate Dr. John Matthews in Los Angeles on the subject of Anglo-Israelism.

Wallace remained always above becoming part of any faction in the church. He was very clear in stating his positions on issues with which others disagreed. One of these views was his understanding of the work of the Holy Spirit. He steadfastly opposed any view that in any way would indicate a direct operation of the Holy Spirit apart from the Scriptures. He also opposed the so-called "dynamic equivalence" modern paraphrase versions of the Bible. He defended the reliability of the Authorized (King James) Version.

He was the author of more than a dozen books. In addition to *God's Prophetic Word*, he also wrote *The Instrumental Music Question*, which is a definitive answer to the use of mechanical instruments of music in Christian worship. *Bulwarks of the Faith* is a classic work which exposes and answers denominational doctrines. He also wrote commentaries on the Revelation, and on Romans, Galatians, and Ephesians (one volume). His sermon books include, *The Gospel for Today*, *The Certified Gospel*, and *Number One Gospel Sermons.* Wallace also wrote: *The Christian and Government, The Sermon on the Mount and the Civil State, The Story of the Norris-Wallace Debate, The Neal-Wallace Debate, A Review of the New Versions, Current Issues,* and *The Mission and Medium of the Holy Spirit.* A compilation of his sermon outlines was also published as well as a compilation of his articles from the years he served as editor of various papers. That book is titled, *The Present Truth.*

The Hardeman Tabernacle Meetings

On September 6, 1921, a meeting was held at the Grandview Heights church of Christ in Nashville to discuss the possibility of a cooperative evangelistic meeting for the city of Nashville. It was decided that N.B. Hardeman, who was reaching the height of his ability as a preacher, should be the one to conduct the meeting with C.M. Pullias leading the singing.

The Tabernacle Sermons at the Ryman Auditorium became the highlight of Hardeman's preaching career. A series of five meetings in all were held in Nashville, Tennessee.

The first meeting occurred from March 28-April 16, 1922. Both *The Tennessean* and the *Nashville Banner* newspapers reported on the meeting, which in turn was picked up by many regional and national papers. It is believed that Hardeman preached to an aggregate total audience of 160,000 people during this meeting. 200 were baptized.

The second meeting occurred from April 1-April 22, 1923. It is believed that Hardeman preached to an aggregate total attendance of 190,000 people for this meeting. 100 were baptized.

The third meeting occurred March 18-April 1, 1928. It is believed that 120,000 people attended these meetings.

The fourth meeting lasted from October 16-October 31, 1938. And the fifth and final meeting took place in the War Memorial building and Central church building during November 1-8, 1945.

The success of these meetings led to similar meetings being conducted in Texas. G.C. Brewer preached a series of lessons in a cooperative effort in Fort Worth, Texas, in 1927. This meeting was conducted in the First Baptist Church building, because of its enormous size, and lasted from September 18-October 2. You will find these sermons printed in a book titled, "Brewer's Sermons."

Foy E. Wallace Jr., also conducted two great meetings in the Houston Music Hall in 1945 and 1946. These meetings are recorded in the books, "God's Prophetic Word" and "Bulwarks of the Faith."

Unity Efforts

By the 1920's, the Christian Church's separation from the Disciples was a foregone conclusion. Perhaps this led to some unity efforts which were made with the churches of Christ. Three occurred in the 1930's. In 1937 a meeting was held in Cincinnati. In 1938 one was held in Detroit. And in May, 1939 the last one was held in Indianapolis. H. Leo Boles was called upon to address the assembly. His speech can be found on the internet and obtained in tract form. Let us look at the conclusion to his speech.

"All who truly believe in Christ, who take the New Testament without any addition or subtraction as a guide, and love the Lord can be united in one holy and happy brotherhood without any sacrifice of truth or conscience. If man's wisdom can guide in the service of God, it is as good as the wisdom of God; to make services based on the opinions of man a part of the worship of God is to place them on an equality with the blood-sealed appointments of Christ; to do such is to make the wisdom and authority of man equal with the wisdom and authority of God. All who do this count the blood of Christ, which seals the covenant, unholy—that is without sanctifying efficacy. If service, based on man's opinions and unsealed by the blood of Christ, is acceptable to God, it is equal to that service rendered through the blood-sealed appointments, and hence the blood is of no avail; it is unholy; and it does not consecrate nor sanctify the service sealed by it. If any service not authorized by the word of God, not sealed by the blood of Christ, is acceptable to God, then that authority and blood are not needed to render any service acceptable. Hence, to introduce those things not authorized by God and not sealed by the blood of Christ is to declare the sanction of the Holy Spirit and the seal of the blood not necessary.

"There is but one pathway to unity among God's people; there is but one rule that can make us one in Christ Jesus; only one way that can bring salvation to the world. All must exalt the supremacy of the word of God and keep opinions private; no one should propagate his opinions in "the areas of silence," but acknowledge the leadership of Christ and love each other as brethren in order to enjoy Christian unity. So let each one lay aside all opinions, ways, inventions, devices, practices, organizations, creeds, confessions, names, manner of work, except those plainly presented and clearly required in the New Testament. Let all determine to do nothing in religion, save that plainly taught in the scripture and ask his brother to accept nothing that God has not required. Let all do faithfully just what God has required, and let all do this in the way approved by God, and unity is the inevitable result and no "conference" or "unity meeting" is needed. This will reduce all religious worship and service to its original divine simplicity and purity, and will restore to it its original efficacy and power to save. In this simplicity and purity of worship, and in perfect harmony with the will of God, the richest blessings of God will be ours. Faith unites men to God and one another; opinions sever them from God and one another; opinions are the occasions of endless strife and bitterness. Brethren, let us not be deceived; let us not have a misguided zeal for unity that blinds us to the only way which leads to God and unity. When Martin Luther was summoned by imperial authority before the Diet of Worms and asked to recant what he had said, he closed his speech with these immortal words: 'Unless you confute me by arguments drawn from the scripture, I cannot and will not recant anything; for my conscience is a captive to God's word, and it is neither safe nor right to go against conscience. Here I take My stand- I can do no otherwise. So help me God Amen!'"

Great Debates from This Period

Many outstanding debates took place in this period. Many outstanding debaters lived through these years. And, much of their influence, reasoning, and argumentation is still alive in the churches of Christ today.

The **Hardeman-Boswell** discussion was between N.B. Hardeman and Ira Boswell (a Christian Church preacher). The subject discussed was instrumental music in worship. It was conducted in the Ryman Auditorium in Nashville from May 31-June 5, 1923.

Not long after this debate the Christian Church lost its enthusiasm for debating this issue.

The **Hardeman-Bogard** debate took place in Little Rock, Arkansas, on April 19-22, 1938. This debate covered a wide variety of issues, such as: the work of the Holy Spirit, Baptism, the establishment of the church, and the possibility of apostasy. Hardeman was at his best for this debate and so was Ben Bogard. Bogard was the champion Missionary Baptist debater of his era.

The **Wallace-Neal** discussion took place twice between Foy E. Wallace, Jr., and Charles Neal of the Christian Church. They debated in 1933 in Winchester, Kentucky, and Chattanooga, Tennessee. The debate that was printed occurred in Winchester from January 2-6, 1933. The discussion centers on the 1,000 years of Revelation chapter 20. The debate in Chattanooga took place June 6-9, 1933.

The **Wallace-Norris** debate occurred November 5-8, 1934, in Fort Worth, Texas. Frank Norris preached for the First Baptist Church in that city and had made the challenge to debate. The subjects discussed were the 1,000 year reign of Christ, the Return of the Jews and their conversion as a nation to Christ, once saved always saved, and baptism.

Some controversy occurred, however, over the transcribing of the debate for publication. Wallace was notified that he would not be allowed to have his own stenographer and that Norris would provide one. During the debate, Wallace noticed that the stenographer was not copying his words when he spoke. He also noticed that Norris was simply handing him his manuscripts, rather than having his speeches copied as they were spoken.

When the time came for the debate to go to print, Wallace could see that it was not the same debate that took place, as many words were added and many omitted. Legal actions followed to keep this "version" of the debate from being printed. For a more complete picture of what occurred, read "The Story of the Wallace – Norris Debate."

The **Brewer-Lindsay** debate took place in Memphis on April 2, 1928. Ben Lindsay was a Memphis judge who had traveled the country debating the lawfulness of "Companionate Marriage." Brewer felt the judge's writings needed to be answered from a Christian perspective. This debate has an odd format as Brewer allowed Lindsay to have the first and last speech.

The **Boles-Boll** debate of 1928, as we have noted, was first printed in the *Gospel Advocate* and *Word and Work*. It was later published in book form.

Timeline of Events 1921-1940

➢ **March 28-April 16, 1922** – The first Ryman Meeting with Hardeman occurs.

➢ **April 1-April 22, 1923** – The second Ryman Meeting with Hardeman occurs.

➢ **May 31-June 5, 1923** – Hardeman–Boswell debate occurs in Nashville.

➢ **December, 1925** – The Central congregation in downtown Nashville begins a daily radio broadcast. Today it is the longest running and oldest religious broadcast in America.

➢ **March 21, 1926** – The Chapel Avenue congregation in Nashville opens the Christian Home for the Aged.

➢ **September 18-October 2, 1927** – G.C. Brewer preaches a series of lessons on Christ at the First Baptist Church building in Fort Worth.

➢ **March 18-April 1, 1928** – The third Ryman Meeting with Hardeman occurs.

➢ **April 2, 1928** – Brewer-Lindsay debate occurs in Memphis.

➢ **Dec. 4, 1928** – G.C. Brewer preaches to "one of the greatest audiences ever assembled" in Detroit, on the subject of "Evolution and Its Relation to Christianity."

➢ **January 2-6, 1933** – The Wallace-Neal debate occurs in Winchester, Kentucky.

➢ **June 6-9, 1933** – The second Wallace-Neal debate occurs in Chattanooga.

➢ **November 5-8, 1934** – Wallace-Norris debate occurs in Fort Worth.

- ➤ **April 19-22, 1938** – Hardeman-Bogard debate occurs in Little Rock.

- ➤ **October 16-October 31, 1938** – The fourth Ryman Meeting with Hardeman occurred.

- ➤ **May, 1939** – H. Leo Boles delivers a speech on unity between the Christian Church and the churches of Christ in Indianapolis.

Chapter Nine

Years of Growth for the Church

1941-1960

In 1945, the U.S. was reported to have had 600,000 members of the church in 8,000 congregations. From 1945-1950 it is said that the church increased by 50,000, increasing the body by 8% to a total of 650,000. 750 congregations were started bringing the total to 8,750 for an increase of 9%. During this period the nation grew by 11%.

From 1950-1955, it was again reported that the church grew by roughly 50,000 members for an 8% increase. In 1955 the total membership was 700,000 in 9,000 congregations. As previously noted, it was not until 1955 that the church recovered from the loss of membership due to the Christian Church split. 250 congregations were added at a rate of 3%. During this time the nation grew by an increase of 8%.

The years from 1955-1960 were reported to be a considerable period of growth in the church. Membership was reported to have increased by 100,000 to a total of 800,000. The church grew by 14% while the nation grew by 9%. 250 new congregations were established to bring the total to 9,250. The number of congregations increased during this time by 3%.

Prominent Leaders

 **Batsell Barrett Baxter** (1916-1982) has to be considered one of the prominent preachers of this era and the years to come. Baxter began preaching in 1933 at Nashville, Tennessee. He also served as head of the Speech Department and later of the Department of Bible at David Lipscomb College.

Baxter preached for the Trinity Lane Church in Nashville from 1946-51. He served the Hillsboro Church as its regular preacher from 1951 until his retirement in 1980.

132

Brother Baxter also wrote a number of books including *Heart of the Yale Lectures*, and *Speaking for the Master*.

Brother Baxter was the first preacher for the "Herald of Truth" television program in August, 1959. Later he became a regular speaker for the radio series of "Herald of Truth." Batsell Barrett Baxter died March 31, 1982. He was 65.

 **Gus Nichols** (1892-1975) must also be considered during this period. Gus Nichols was born in Walker County, Alabama, on January 12, 1892. In August 1909, C.A. Wheeler conducted a meeting at the Iron Mountain School. Because no one else was available and because of the high esteem in which he was held by the community, Gus Nichols, while still a Baptist, was asked to lead the singing during the meeting. Brother Wheeler baptized Gus Nichols during that meeting. He attended at White's Chapel, New River, and Carbon Hill churches of Christ.

In May 1916 Gus Nichols began preaching at the Iron Mountain School. On the night of May 27, 1917, a tornado blew away the Nichols's home. Gus Nichols was reading or had been reading Brents' *The Gospel Plan of Salvation* by the light of a kerosene lamp when the storm struck. He determined, with his wife's firm support, to become a full-time preacher after this incident.

In 1919 Gus Nichols moved his family to Berry, Alabama, to study under Hal P. McDonald at Alabama Christian College. In February 1924 Nichols moved to Cordova, Alabama, to preach. He remained there until the early days of 1926 when he moved to Millport, Alabama, where he remained until December 29, 1932, when he moved to Jasper.

In 1933, brother Nichols came to Jasper to begin his work as a preacher. He continued until his death Sunday, November 16,

1975, at his residence. For forty-two years he conducted a training class on Friday night during the winter months. Hundreds of preachers and elders attended these sessions. He also had a daily radio program that maintained a large listening audience.

Franklin Camp (1915-1991) began to preach in 1935. His father and grandfather were both preachers before him. Brother Camp did most of his located preaching in Alabama. He had a tremendous influence in this state, perhaps second only to Gus Nichols.

In addition to being a great gospel preacher, brother Camp was also a tremendous writer. His volume on "The Work of the Holy Spirit in Redemption" is a classic in that field of study.

W.A. Bradfield (1910-1972) was an outstanding evangelist who must also be considered. W.A. Bradfield was born December 27, 1910, at Wildersville, near Lexington, in west Tennessee. He obeyed the gospel when he was fifteen and began preaching in his home community at Christian Chapel when he was twenty-eight.

After graduating from Freed-Hardeman (when it was a two-year college), he received his undergraduate degree from Memphis State University (now the University of Memphis). He then received the Master of Arts degree from Peabody College in Nashville. During the next ten years (1939-49), along with his preaching, he was a school principal.

In the fall of 1949 brother Bradfield began working with Freed-Hardeman College. He remained there until his death in 1972.

During the decade of the 1960s it is possible that as many as 10,000 persons publically responded to his sermons. Of the many gospel meetings he held, 19 had as many as 100 public responses; and two meetings had 99 responses.

His biography is titled, "You've Been a Good Brother, Willie." The book also includes his sermon outlines.

 **Guy N. Woods** (1908-1993) had an influence in the church for much of the Twentieth Century. He was an outstanding author, debater, editor of the *Gospel Advocate*, and evangelistic preacher. A recent biography has been written about him titled, "Over the Vast Horizon."

Guy N. Woods was born September 26, 1908, in Vardeman, Mississippi. When he was just a small child, the family moved back to their earlier home in west Tennessee at Holladay in Benton County. At the age of seventeen he was baptized into Christ by J.W. Grant on August 24, 1926. His brother, G.E. Woods, age thirteen, obeyed the gospel at the same time.

The next month, on his eighteenth birthday, Guy N. Woods preached his first sermon at Holladay. At about the same time he entered Freed-Hardeman College. After graduation from college, he preached full time for the church at Tompkinsville, Kentucky, and then in Texas for churches of Christ at Post, Kirkland, Wellington, and Lubbock. Starting in 1945 Woods devoted his full time to preaching in gospel meetings all over America. At times he had hundreds of meetings booked years in advance.

Woods scheduled the first week in February each year to be in Henderson, Tennessee, to conduct the "Open Forum" at the Freed-Hardeman College Lectureship. Two volumes of the Open Forum have been printed.

Guy N. Woods was known for his skill in debate. Many of his debates were printed. His debates varied in subject and opponents.

Woods always taught the truth in a masterful way during these debates.

Brother Woods passed away in Nashville, Tennessee, December 8, 1993. The funeral took place at his home church at Holladay, Tennessee.

H.A. Dixon (1904-1969) replaced N.B. Hardeman as president of Freed-Hardeman College in 1950. He remains one of the most respected Christians of the Twentieth Century. He is fondly remembered for his guidance and soundness at FHC until his untimely death in 1969. If not for brother Dixon's leadership, FHC might have closed in the early 1950's.

To many, brother H.A. Dixon remains the ideal Christian college leader. He considered himself first to be a gospel preacher and he was determined never to associate with anything that would compromise his convictions as a Christian – even if it meant standing up to the regional accrediting bodies.

Perhaps his finest contribution to FHC was a third year Bible program for gospel preachers. Many faithful preachers benefited tremendously from this extra year of education. When the accrediting body attempted to stop this third year program on the basis of its uniqueness, brother Dixon threatened to remove the school from the association. The association recanted its threats and the third year program remained intact.

George Benson (1898-1991) was president of Harding College. Benson is remembered for his strong opposition to communism and his advocacy for conservative government. The following is taken from the restorationmovement.com:

136

On May 15, 1941, he appeared before the Ways and Means Committee of the U.S. House of Representatives as the committee was holding public hearings on a proposed tax bill to help finance the defense effort in World War II.

His speech made national headlines. Some newspapers printed the entire text. The Chicago Journal of Commerce offered reprints for a dollar per 100 and received orders for 300,000 copies. Banks, insurance companies, railroad companies and others reprinted the speech until some 2,000,000 copies were in circulation.

In that speech, Benson told members of the committee that they should not think of raising taxes until they had eliminated all unnecessary expenses of the government. He did not deal in generalities. He specified agencies and projects that could be abolished or cut down to size.

The Civilian Conservation Corps was one. He pointed out that it had been created during the Depression to provide jobs, but with defense plants springing up over the country and with navy yards advertising for workers. There was no longer any need for make work projects. The same was true with the National Youth Administration and the Works Progress Administration.

As he continued ticking off savings that could be made, he gained the attention of the members of that committee. At the conclusion of the speech, committee members violated their own standing rule of never applauding a speaker. They gave him a rousing ovation. Within two years, the WPA, the CCC and the NYA were all gone. Other savings he had recommended were put into effect. The Tax Foundation of America honored him at a banquet at the Waldorf Astoria Hotel in New York on Dec. 3, 1941. The president of the foundation praised him as being the most effective speaker and influence in the nation in achieving results for sane governmental economy.

 **B.C. Goodpasture** (1895-1977) was the influential editor of the *Gospel Advocate* during this period. Goodpasture began preaching October 18, 1912, at Holly Springs, Tennessee. Places where he did full time local work were: Shelbyville, Tennessee; West End Church in Atlanta, Georgia, 1920-1927; Poplar Street Church in Florence, Alabama, one year; Seminole Avenue Church in Atlanta until 1939; Hillsboro Church of Christ in Nashville, Tennessee, 12 years. He held meetings in 20 States.

Goodpasture became one of the most knowledgeable collectors of both good and rare books in his lifetime. In 1932, the *Atlanta Journal* featured Goodpasture as a collector of rare books and this continued to the end of his life. Goodpasture's private library included 10,000 volumes.

Willard Collins (1915-2007) was also a very strong preacher of this period. He began preaching in 1934 in Farmington, Tennessee. After 1955 he preached by appointment and over a dozen gospel meetings per year. In 1949 he preached a gospel meeting at Old Hickory, Tennessee. In that meeting there were 166 responses, including 111 baptisms.

According to *Preachers of Today*, Vol. 5, as of December, 1980 Collins had baptized 6,793 people, and received a total of 12,223 responses, including 5,430 restorations as a result of his preaching and teaching. He had great success in the ministry. His booming voice and understanding of the scriptures kept his audiences spellbound.

Nashville churches of Christ held the first event in the Nashville Municipal Auditorium when they had Willard Collins conduct an area-wide evangelistic meeting from October 7-14, 1962.

For many years he served David Lipscomb University in a number of different ways. From June 1, 1946 to August 31, 1977 he served as vice-president of the college, a total of 31 years. After the departure of President Athens Clay Pullias, the board of Trustees unanimously decided to appoint Collins president of the college September 1, 1977. (from therestorationmovement.com)

 **Ira North** (1922-1984) became very influential in the Nashville area especially. He was the minister for the Madison congregation, which became the largest congregation of churches of Christ in the world, numbering over 4,000.

Amazingly, brother North was never a full-time preacher for the Madison congregation. He taught Bible and related subjects at David Lipscomb College and also served as editor for the *Gospel Advocate*. Brother North also had a very popular television Bible study program titled "Amazing Grace."

James Burton Coffman (1905-2006) gave us one of the best one-man commentary sets on the whole Bible ever written. Coffman conducted hundreds of gospel meetings throughout the U.S. and, at one count, baptized more than 3,000 souls.

 **Rex Turner, Sr.** (1913-2001) co-founded the two Montgomery schools affiliated with the church, now known as Faulkner University and Amridge University. He was a longtime minister of the Panama Street Church of Christ in Montgomery (at least 24 years).

Leslie G. Thomas (1895-1988) was one of the most prolific writers of his era. He produced some of the best sermon outline and full-content sermon books in a time known for the publication of great sermon books. In total, he produced over a dozen volumes on a variety of themes, while also compiling J.W. McGarvey's class notes.

Leroy Brownlow (1914-2002), like many from this period, had already established his influence by this time. His book, "Why I Am a Member of the Church of Christ" has sold over one million copies world-wide. Brother Brownlow wrote over thirty volumes in his life on a variety of Bible related themes, including many fine sermon books.

Brownlow preached in a cooperative meeting of 27 congregations in Tulsa, Oklahoma, which marked the opening of the Tulsa Civic Center and averaged 8,500 in attendance per night. There were 190 responses, including 83 baptisms.

For 22 years he labored with the Polytechnic church of Christ in Fort Worth, Texas. Polytechnic gave 200 members, two elders, 16 teachers and assistant teachers to start the Meadowbrook congregation. The remarkable thing is the very next year Polytechnic had a higher average attendance than the year before!

They gave 200 members to start Eastland Street. They helped to start Vickery Boulevard all over again after the former group moved to Mitchell Boulevard. They assisted in establishing Flamingo Road and Linwood congregations. Also, they bought and paid for the prime location and set aside $160,000 to start the Brentwood church, now Bridgewood.

Polytechnic was also the first church of Christ in the world to be on television. (*Firm Foundation*, Vol. 118, No. 7; July, 2003, Houston, Texas, by Nobel Patterson)

James D. Bales (1915-1995) was a Harding Bible Professor, author, and preacher. Brother Bales was the most prolific writer of his time among his brethren. He was at the forefront of opposing liberalism and communism. Sadly, brother Bales was at the center of the divorce and remarriage controversy that is still turbulent in churches of Christ. This is sad because Bales did so much good and wrote so many very good books and articles. Yet, his reputation has been forever injured among brethren because of his teaching on this topic.

Bales was not alone in believing what he did, but he was perhaps the most vocal. Bales believed that Jesus' comments on marriage, divorce, and remarriage did not apply to non-Christians, and that therefore whatever marriage they were in when they obeyed the gospel, it was acceptable to God.

Perhaps the best debate ever conducted on this issue was his debate with **Roy C. Deaver**. This was a written debate that began around 1980.

Otis Gatewood (1911-1999) was a pioneer in mission work in Germany and Eastern Europe especially. Gatewood's book *You Can Do Personal Work* remains a classic work on personal evangelism.

In 2013 the *Lubbock Avalanche-Journal* reported a 1992 meeting between Gatewood and Mikhail Gorbachev. In the context of the meeting Gatewood had accompanied food shipments to Russian orphans and elderly people from churches of Christ in Texas. During the meeting Gorbachev claimed that he was "indeed a Christian and had been baptized by his grandfather in the Volga River many years before."

The Jule Miller Filmstrips

Jule Miller (1925-2000) was the right man at the right time in our history. Using advanced technology for his day, he gave us a set of film-strips which led to the conversion of literally tens of thousands of souls worldwide. He has paved the way for what brethren are doing today through DVD's.

In 1956, Jule, along with Texas H. Stevens, produced a series of film strips that were to be used for evangelism purposes. They were called the "Visualized Bible Study." Today it is produced in numerous languages in many different countries.

The *Gospel Advocate* named Jule Miller as one of the 20th century's most influential men in contributing to the growth of the Lord's church.

Area-Wide Campaigns

Foy E. Wallace Jr., held two notable meetings at the Music Hall in Houston during the 1940's. In the first meeting of January 21-28, 1945, he addressed the issue of pre-millennialism. These sermons have been recorded in the book "God's Prophetic Word" which stands as the masterpiece of the a-millennial position from the Twentieth Century.

The second meeting was conducted the following January and addressed the dogmas of Protestantism and Roman Catholicism.

These sermons were also recorded in a book which is titled, "Bulwarks of the Faith."

In May of 1956, Batsell Barrett Baxter conducted an area-wide campaign in Lubbock, TX. More than 30,000 people attended these sessions, which were conducted in the recently built Municipal Auditorium of that city. The sermons preached at the Lubbock Bible Forum are recorded in the book, "If I Be Lifted Up."

Willard Collins also held a similar meeting in the recently constructed Municipal Auditorium in Nashville. In fact, I believe this meeting was the first event ever held in that building.

New Colleges Established

The **Nashville Christian Institute** was a segregated school that operated from 1940-1967. Marshall Keeble served as the school's president from 1942-1958.

The **Montgomery Bible School** (now Faulkner University) began on Ann Street in Montgomery, Alabama in 1942. Rex Turner and Leonard Johnson served as the co-founding presidents of the school. In 1953, the school was renamed Alabama Christian College, and eleven years later, the present property on the Atlanta Highway was purchased. In 1985, the college was renamed Faulkner University in honor of longtime supporter, trustee, and chairman of the board, Dr. James Faulkner of Bay Minnette, Alabama.

Florida College was conceived in 1942, its charter drafted in 1944, and its first students enrolled in 1946. From its beginning the College has remained independent of church affiliation and has operated without financial support either from churches or from the government.

Oklahoma Christian College began with L.R. Wilson serving as the first president of then Central Christian College in Bartlesville, Oklahoma.

In September of 1950, Central Christian College opened its doors to about 90 students. In 1954, James Baird became the president of the college. Central Christian later moved from Bartlesville to Oklahoma City.

In 1974, J. Terry Johnson became the next president of the school. In 1981, he became publisher of the *Christian Chronicle*, a newspaper for members of the churches of Christ. The circulation of the paper grew from 3,600 to more than 100,000 and brought great recognition to Oklahoma Christian from its church constituency. Dr. Baird suffered a debilitating stroke in 1990 and died in February 1998.

North Central Christian College (now Rochester College) began in rural Rochester, Michigan. In September of 1959, the college opened as North Central Christian College, retaining that name until 1961, when it became known as Michigan Christian College.

In 1997, the college changed its name from Michigan Christian College to Rochester College.

York College in York, Nebraska, began to be operated by members of the churches of Christ in the fall of 1956. York College was founded on August 26, 1890, by the United Brethren Church in conjunction with York citizens who wanted a church-related college. An agreement had existed from the school's beginning that control of the school would pass to the City of York should the governing body ever decide to close the college. Because of this, the city took control of the property, and the corporate structure, which has remained continuous since 1890, was transferred to members of the churches of Christ in 1956.

The new administration reopened York College in fall 1956 as a senior college with 89 students. The college has grown from only four major buildings in 1956, to a campus of 17 major facilities on 50 acres that serve the needs of a growing student body. Fall enrollment is typically between 400 and 500 students, coming from about 30 states and several countries.

Lubbock Christian College was established in 1957. In 1954 the State of Texas approved the operation of a private educational institution for students from kindergarten through college. An elementary school was established that year, and a junior college was added in 1957.

F. W. Mattox was the founding president. LCU received accreditation as a senior college in 1972. Advancement to university status came in the fall of 1987. F.W. Mattox is best remembered for his classic book, *The Eternal Kingdom*, which pertains to church history.

Fort Worth Christian College was a two-year junior college located in Fort Worth, Texas. Roy Deaver was the first president of the college. The college began classes in the fall of 1959 and expanded annually. Thomas B. Warren was appointed president that year. Claude A. Guild succeeded Warren in 1961. Curtis E. Ramey served as president in 1965.

Due to financial difficulties Fort Worth Christian College ceased to exist in 1971 and became a branch of Abilene Christian College (now Abilene Christian University). Thomas A. Shaver was executive dean. In 1973 the branch merged with the former Christian College of the Southwest to form the ACC Metrocenter. By 1976 the Metrocenter had become Abilene Christian University

145

in Dallas (later Amber University, now Amberton University), and classes were discontinued at the Fort Worth campuses.

Ohio Valley Christian College (now Ohio Valley University) is located in Parkersburg, West Virginia. On September 14, 1960, the college opened with classes being offered at South Parkersburg Church of Christ. In 1963 the South Campus opened on 133 acres between Parkersburg and Vienna which had been purchased in 1958.

In 1994 the college doubled its campus size with the purchase of 134 acres and a four storied building from the Roman Catholic Diocese of Wheeling-Charleston, West Virginia. This separate campus became the North Campus. In 2005 the college changed its name to Ohio Valley University.

Timeline of Events 1941-1960

➤ **January 21-28, 1945** – Foy E. Wallace Jr., preaches at the Houston Music Hall on the subject of pre-millennialism.

➤ **January 1946** – Foy E. Wallace holds a second meeting at the Houston Music Hall. This time the subjects are Protestant and Catholic dogmas.

➤ **July 2-5, 1946** – Guy N. Woods debates A.U. Nunnery on baptism and the possibility of Apostasy.

➤ **October 6-9, 1947** – James D. Bales debates Woosley Teller on the existence of God. This is considered by many to be one of the best accounts of a Christian defending God's existence against an atheist.

➤ **February 1950** – N.B. Hardeman is fired from FHC. H.A. Dixon becomes the next president. Under Dixon the college would grow from 350 to over 750 students.

➤ **1952** – The Herald of Truth moves to the oversight of the Highland church of Christ in Abilene, Texas

➤ **June 30-July 4, 1952** – G.K. Wallace debates W. Carl Ketcherside on the non-institutional question.

➤ **July 23-26, 1952** – Thomas B. Warren debates L.S. Ballard on the subjects of baptism and apostasy.

➤ **January 3-6, 1956** – The Porter-Woods debate is conducted in Memphis.

➤ **May 1956** – Batsell Barrett Baxter conducts the Lubbock Bible Forum.

➤ **November 18-23, 1957** – The Cogdill-Woods debate is held in Birmingham, Alabama.

Chapter Ten

The Non-Institutional Controversy

In the 1950s and 1960s churches divided over what some perceived to be matters of judgment and others perceived to be matters of divinely-specified doctrine.

The controversy first started when **G.C. Brewer, N.B. Hardeman**, and a few others began calling for churches to support the colleges from their treasuries. Debates occurred in the pages of the *Bible Banner* in the 1930s and 1940s. The issue was also discussed in the *Firm Foundation* in 1947. Men like Brewer and Hardeman were in favor of churches supporting colleges, and men such as **Foy E. Wallace, Jr., Cled Wallace**, and **R.L. Whiteside** opposed the idea. Brewer and Hardeman believed that support of the college and orphan home stood or fell together; whereas Wallace and co. believe them to be separate issues.

The brotherhood had been badly burned by the missionary society controversy and, therefore, anything that appeared to move in that direction, even slightly, was critically considered. On the issue of churches supporting colleges, it is true that prior to WWII this really was not much of an issue. For the most part, the colleges did not ask and the churches did not give. Churches generally understood the work of the church to be under the headings of benevolence, evangelism, and edification.

Church Cooperation

A radio and television broadcast titled "The Herald of Truth" was also placed at the center of controversy during this period. The program was overseen by the Highland Avenue church in Abilene, Texas. Other congregations gave to Highland Avenue to support the work. Thus, the question of congregational autonomy was raised. It was argued that the Bible does not provide an example of one congregation overseeing a work that is the product of many congregations' support. It was called a "sponsoring church" arrangement.

On the other hand, brethren in favor of the idea pointed out that many congregations in the Bible once gave to the Jerusalem church in order to help victims of a great famine that had afflicted the area (cf. Acts 21:17). The Jerusalem church thus oversaw a work for which many congregations had donated.

Various Other Issues Discussed

During this period, a number of other issues also began to be discussed among brethren. A few of these discussions became heated and led to the division of many congregations. Such issues include:

➢ "Sunday School" and individual Bible classes
➢ Individual communion cups
➢ Eating meals in the church building
➢ Full-time "located" ministers
➢ Women's head coverings
➢ Helping Christians only from the church treasury
➢ Weddings and funerals in the church building

Because the division in the church involved more than just a discussion of which institutions to support, but centered upon whether things as individual communion cups were acceptable, the disparaging title "Anti" was given to congregations and preachers opposed to these ideas. These brethren prefer to be called "conservative" while referring to brethren who disagree with the disparaging title of "liberal" or "digressive."

Preachers Involved

As with the division over instruments of music in worship and the missionary society, prominent preachers and popular religious

151

journals were at the forefront of the non-institutional division as well. Men like Yater Tant (the son of J.D. Tant) and Roy Cogdill used the *Gospel Guardian* as a means of propagating their views before the brotherhood. Also, men like W. Curtis Porter, W. Carl Ketcherside, and James Parker Miller were actively debating these things whenever they could. Alabama preacher John T. Lewis was probably the most respected patriarch of this movement. His biography is titled, "He Looked for a City."

Guy N. Woods and G.K. Wallace were their chief opponents on the debater's platform. E.R. Harper also led a relentless campaign to stop this movement. B.C. Goodpasture even called for churches to boycott using preachers who held these views. He also closed the pages of the *Gospel Advocate* to any proponent of these views.

Non-Institutional Preachers

John T. Lewis (1876-1967) was a graduate of Nashville Bible School in 1906. He was also a staff writer for the *Gospel Advocate* for many years. Perhaps his greatest written work is the book "The Voice of the Pioneers on Instrumental Music and Societies."

Brother Lewis had a great part in planting many congregations in the Birmingham area. His biography is titled, "He Looked for a City."

W. Curtis Porter (1897-1960) began his long preaching career in 1914, at the age of seventeen. One year later he conducted his first debate with D.N. Jackson (Baptist). Porter wrote several books and contributed articles to many publications. He participated in seventy-seven debates (several of which were published), and preached in every state of the union.

152

Roy Cogdill (1907-1985) along with Porter was a co-editor of the *Gospel Guardian*. He, like Porter, was a very active writer among brotherhood publications. Perhaps his best-remembered and best-used book is titled "The New Testament Church" which contains a number of sermon outlines on the subject. He is also remembered for the debates in which he participated with men like Guy N. Woods and Ben Bogard (Baptist).

Yater Tant (1908-1997) was the son of J. D. Tant. Along with Roy Cogdill, he edited the *Gospel Guardian*. He was also among the first to debate the issues in discussions in Lufkin and Abilene, Texas with E.R. Harper. He preached in Texas and in the Birmingham area primarily.

W. Carl Ketcherside (1908-1989) was a key figure early in the non-institutional ranks. Ketcherside conducted numerous debates with preachers such as Rue Porter, G.C. Brewer, G.K. Wallace, and Flavil L. Colley on various points of disagreement.

After serving as a missionary to Ireland in the 1950s, Ketcherside decided to dedicate himself to promoting what he believed to be unity through doctrinal tolerance and openness. He stopped debating. His paper, *Mission Messenger*, promoted tolerance among all believers. He also participated in unity meetings with churches using instrumental music and advocated open fellowship with all claiming to be believers in Christ.

Ketcherside, along with some other non-institutional preachers, went from being extremely restrictive in his fellowship to being ultra-inclusive. Doctrine ceased to be a means to unity; and only faith in Christ was considered to be his test of fellowship. Ketcherside became a key figure in the "Change Agent Movement" of the 1970s and 80s.

Leroy Garrett (1918-2015) followed the same path as his friend W. Carl Ketcherside. He began in the non-institutional ranks only to become one of the leaders in the "Change Agent Movement" among churches of Christ in the latter part of the 20th century.

Garrett was a distinguished scholar, holding a ThM from Princeton and a PhD from Harvard. He was an author, editor, and professor.

H.E. Phillips (1916-2000) and **James P. Miller** (1915-1978) edited *Searching the Scriptures*. Both of these men were very capable preachers and writers. In 1957, they began publishing the *Florida Newsletter* which soon became the *Southeastern Newsletter*. They launched a full-size periodical in January, 1960, and called it *Searching the Scriptures*. For a full decade their names appeared as co-editors. Connie W. Adams latter became the editor.

Bennie Lee Fudge (1914-1972) played a large part in the beginning of Athens Bible School (1943) in Athens, Alabama and founded the CEI Bookstore in Athens. Limestone County, Alabama has many non-institutional churches in large part because of the influence of Bennie Lee Fudge.

A.C. Grider (1912-1990) was considered a champion debater among the non-institutional people. He once affirmed the proposition that it would be sinful to take one cent from the church treasury to feed a starving orphan.

Florida College became associated with the non-institutional brethren. **James R. Cope** left Freed-Hardeman College to become the president of that school following L.R. Wilson. Homer Hailey would join him on the faculty.

 **Homer Hailey** (1903-2000) was a professor at Abilene Christian before going to Florida College. Hailey began preaching in Buffalo Gap, Texas, in 1927. He served as minister for churches in Texas, California, Hawaii, Florida and Arizona and preached in meetings for hundreds of churches of Christ throughout the United States.

He taught Bible at Abilene Christian College for 13 years between 1934 and 1951. He served for 22 years as vice president and head of the Bible department at Florida Christian College in Temple Terrace, Florida, and then retired to Tucson, Arizona in the spring of 1973. After his retirement, Hailey became an even more prolific writer.

Institutional Preachers

 **E.R. Harper** (1897-1986) began preaching in 1924. He would preach for the next sixty years. He was the preacher for the Highland church of Christ in Abilene, Texas, where controversy centered upon the "Herald of Truth" arrangement. He wrote several booklets defended the arrangement, answering many of the arguments being made by the non-institutional preachers.

 G.K. Wallace (1903-1988) was a prolific writer for brotherhood journals and as a preacher was in great demand. He debated the non-institutional and "anti" issues as much as anyone in the early going of this movement. He was also an active debater with Christian Church preachers and denominational preachers in general.

155

W.L. Totty (1903-1982) began preaching in Nashville, Tennessee, in 1926 and did not quit preaching until 53 years later when he was unable to continue. For 43 years and three months, he preached in the city of Indianapolis. He  preached for the Southside, Garfield Heights, and Shelbyville Road congregations.

He debated W. Carl Ketcherside on "Bible Colleges and the Orphan Home" in 1942. And, he had many debates with A.C. Grider on the "Orphan Home" issue in 1958, 1963, 1964, 1965, and 1967.

Guy Woods not only had many debates on these issues, but he also used his opportunity as the moderator for the Open Forum at the annual Freed-Hardeman Bible Lectureship to answer many of the arguments being made and settle the minds of brethren who were present. Two debates from this period that are especially noteworthy are the Porter-Woods debate from January 3-6, 1956 in Memphis; and the Cogdill-Woods debate from November 18-23, 1957. This debate was held in Birmingham.

Thomas B. Warren (1920-2000) and **Roy Deaver** (1922-2007) began a paper titled the *Spiritual Sword* in 1958 to answer the arguments being made by non-institutional brethren. The paper would eventually be overseen by the Getwell church of Christ in Memphis, Tennessee. Roy Deaver also later edited a paper titled *Biblical Notes*.

Significant Debates

G.K. Wallace and **W. Carl Ketcherside** debated first in Paragould, Arkansas, June 10 – July 4, 1952. The propositions discussed pertained to full-time evangelists and Christian colleges.

These two men met again in St. Louis, Missouri, October 26 – 30, 1953.

W. Carl Ketcherside also debated **Flavil Colley** in Dallas, Texas, from December 1 – 4, 1953. The issue of that debate was also full-time ministers.

From April 20 – 23, 1954, **Bill Humble** and **Leroy Garrett** debated the issues of located ministers and Christian colleges in Kansas City, Missouri.

Leroy Garrett debated **George DeHoff** from June 1 – 4, 1954, in Nashville, Tennessee. The issue discussed was again full-time ministers being employed by churches.

E.R. Harper debated **Yater Tant** November 27-30, 1955, in Abilene, Texas. Tant was called upon to defend the existence of the *Gospel Guardian* and Harper defended the practice of congregational cooperation.

During January 3 – 6, 1956, **W. Curtis Porter** and **Guy N. Woods** debated the issue of supporting orphan homes and homes for the aged. The debate was conducted in Indianapolis, Indiana.

From November 18 – 23, 1957, **Guy Woods** debated **Roy Cogdill** on the issues of supporting orphan homes and church cooperation. The debate was conducted in Birmingham, Alabama.

With similar propositions as the Woods-Cogdill debate, **Charles Holt** debated **G.K. Wallace** from December 8 – 11, 1959 in Florence, Alabama.

Alan Highers debated **Eural Bingham** on the issue of church benevolence. The debate took place in Corinth, Mississippi from November 20-24, 1967.

Once again **Guy Woods** debated the issue of church benevolence on May 16, 17, 1977 in Suffolk, Virginia. This time he debated **Eugene Britnell**.

Many other debates occurred during and since this time. These are debates which were printed and from which the reader can come to understand the positions being discussed. After the dust settled, an estimated 120,000 members took the non-institutional position and comprised more than 2,000 congregations in the U.S. One college is affiliated with their movement – Florida College in Tampa, Florida.

Chapter Eleven

Changing Times

1961-1980

Seeds of change were sown in America during the 1960s. Anything and everything was being called into question – politics, society, morals, and religion. Just as it took a generation or two to see a fundamental shift in ideology in our society, it took a number of years to realize the effects of change in the church. The doubts of the 1960s brought about the Change Agent Movement of the 1980s.

Two men who figured prominently in the church in this period were **W. Carl Ketcherside** and **Leroy Garrett**. These men were key figures in the non-institutional controversy of the 1950s, and from the 1960s onward they became key figures in the controversy with liberalism. Just as a pendulum on a clock swings from one extreme to the other, so too did these men.

The efforts of Garrett and Ketcherside began by attempting to unite instrumental and non-instrumental churches of Christ. They proposed that as long as agreement was reached on what they considered a "core gospel" disagreement could be overlooked on other doctrines. Of course, the elements of the "core gospel" were to be determined by Ketcherside, Garrett, and company. Eventually, this doctrine led some congregations into ecumenicalism and fellowship with denominations.

In order to achieve such fellowship, Christians had to be convinced that the church of Christ was born out of the American Restoration Movement and that it was just one denomination among many. The desire to restore and become the church of the New Testament had to be abandoned, along with any notion that this was already accomplished.

Ancient landmarks had to be removed. The Holy Spirit had to be seen as "speaking" to these false teachers in a way that He was not speaking to others. A lack of respect for God's word, biblical elderships, and faithful gospel preachers became evident in some

160

of our Christian colleges and larger metropolitan congregations. More and more, Christians began to accept the practice of social drinking, gambling, and immodest dress. Marriage, divorce, and remarriage also became a controversial subject.

Opponents to Change

Many faithful gospel preachers and congregations fought to resist liberalism in the church. The 1972 Freed-Hardeman College Bible Lectureship was dedicated to theme of "The Bible verses Liberalism." Faithful churches and preachers were aware of what was happening and began to speak against such things. They sought to promote awareness among brethren.

Foy E. Wallace, Jr., saw modernism (denial of miracles, etc.) in the modern versions of the Bible and warned brethren and teachers from using them. He observed on many occasions that: "I can remember when a liberal could not be found among us with a fine-toothed comb, but now you could not bale them up with a hay rake."

Ira Y. Rice, Jr., opposed liberalism by reporting on various activities in colleges and congregations. His paper was titled, *Contending for the Faith*. **Roy J. Hearn** also began a publication in 1971 to address liberalism in the church. His paper was titled *First Century Christian*. **Franklin Camp** was co-editor. **Thomas B. Warren** also opposed this movement along with **Garland Elkins** in the *Spiritual Sword*. **Alan Highers** was also an effective writer for this publication while he was the preacher for the Getwell Road church of Christ in Memphis, which oversees the paper.

As liberalism began to spread throughout the colleges and universities associated with the church, congregations began to establish schools of preaching to train gospel preachers.

The School of Preaching Movement

Sunset Bible Institute began in 1962 and is operated by the Sunset congregation in Lubbock, Texas.

 In addition to being an outstanding writer and debater, **Roy Lanier, Sr.** (1899-1980) helped to begin the **Bear Valley Bible Institute**. The Bear Valley Bible Institute began in September of 1965 and is overseen by the Bear Valley church in Denver.

Roy Hearn (1911-2000) helped to begin the **Nashville School of Preaching** as well as the **Memphis School of Preaching**. The Nashville School of Preaching began in February of 1966 and is now overseen by the Crieve Hall congregation in  Nashville. The Memphis School of Preaching began in 1966 at the Getwell congregation and is now overseen by the Forrest Hills congregation outside of Memphis.

Roy Deaver (1922-2007), who also helped to begin the Spiritual Sword and edited Biblical Notes Quarterly, helped to begin the **Brown Trail School of Preaching**. The Brown Trail School of Preaching began in September of 1965 and is overseen by the Brown Trail congregation in Fort Worth, Texas.

The **Florida School of Preaching** began in 1969 in Lakeland, Florida and is currently under a board of directors.

The **East Tennessee School of Preaching** began in 1971 in Knoxville, Tennessee, and is overseen by the Karns church of Christ. It is now called the Southeast Institute of Biblical Studies

The **Southwest School of Preaching** began in 1978 in Austin, Texas, and is overseen by the Southwest congregation.

Soul Winners at Work

A great many soul-winners were at work during this period as well. An estimated 115,000 souls were added to the church from 1960-1965. 250 congregations were believed to be established. The church grew by 14% while the nation grew by 6%. Congregations continued to multiply steadily at a rate of 3%.

From 1965-1970 the growth rate declined to an increase of 1%, but still an estimated 85,000 souls were baptized during this time. It was reported that one thousand congregations were started during this time at an increase of 10%. The church reportedly grew from 915,000 members to 1,000,000 in 10,500 congregations. During this time the nation grew by 10%.

From 1970-1980 the church continued to grow. One source cited that 240,820 souls were added to the church and 2,262 new congregations were established. If true, membership grew by 24% while the nation grew by 10%. An unusually high amount of congregational growth was experienced during this time as congregations multiplied from 10,500 to 12,762 for an increase of 22%. This is recorded as the highest increase of congregational growth for a ten year period since 1906-1916.

Overall growth from 1965 to 1980 was quite substantial. Figures cite that the church grew by 325,820 members and 3,262 congregations. By 1980 there were 1,240,820 members in 12,762 congregations. The church grew by 36% in membership and 34% in congregations for these fifteen years. Truly, this was a period of unprecedented growth in the number of members in the United States.

Only in the period of 1906-1916 were more congregations established in such a short period of time. Even while the world seemed so rebellious, the numbers prove that people were still being attracted by the gospel.

Preachers and Their Works

Thomas B. Warren (1920-2000) was editor of the *Spiritual Sword* for twenty years, beginning with Volume 1, Number 1, in October of 1969 and continuing through Volume 20, Number 4, in July of 1989. He participated in numerous debates and  wrote extensively. One of his most renowned debates was in 1976 with Anthony Flew. He authored a number of books and earned a PhD from Vanderbilt University. His debate with L.S. Ballard (Baptist) is an excellent example of his early work, and remains one of the finest printed debates on the subjects of baptism and the conditional security of the believer. He remained a strong opponent to liberalism throughout his life.

Hugo McCord (1911-2004) was born in New Albany, Mississippi, June 24, 1911 and baptized into Christ by L.L. Brigance, in 1923. He also received a doctorate and was a professor for many years at Oklahoma Christian University.

Hugo McCord preached in Urbana, Illinois; Indianapolis, Indiana; Washington, D.C.; Dallas, Texas; Alexandria, Virginia; Louisville, Kentucky; Bartlesville, Oklahoma; New Orleans, Louisiana; and Midwest City, Oklahoma.

His evangelistic work carried him into forty-two states, and into the following foreign countries: Sierra Leone, Great Britain, Scotland, Ireland, Australia, Tasmania, New Zealand, Indonesia, Japan, the Philippines, Kenya, Malta, Trinidad, Canada, Egypt, Italy, Sweden, and Thailand.

V.P. Black (1918-2007) worked with the Plateau Church of Christ (now Central) in Mobile, Alabama, for forty years (twenty-eight years as their local preacher). During the next twelve years he did evangelistic work under the oversight of the Plateau elders.

At one time, he averaged more than forty-five meetings per year. He began preaching in meetings at the age of twenty. For thirty-two years he conducted from twelve to fifteen meetings per year. In 1965 brother Black preached in a campaign in Mobile, Alabama. There were 269 responses during that meeting. Ninety-eight were baptisms. The same year he preached in a campaign in Summerville, Georgia, with 191 responses. In 1966 he preached in a campaign in Anniston, Alabama with 198 responses. He preached in a meeting for his home congregation with fifty-two baptisms.

Through the years brother Black preached in hundreds of gospel meetings and area-wide campaigns resulting in thousands of baptisms and Christians deciding to rededicate their lives to Christ.

 **Jimmy Allen** was recognized preacher for area-wide meetings during this period. He preached in approximately 50 area-wide campaigns in such cities as Detroit, Dallas, St. Louis, Phoenix, Memphis, Seattle, Denver, Indianapolis, Austin, Amarillo, Charleston, and Parkersburg. He preached in 42 states, Australia, Greece, Lebanon, North Ireland, Japan, Jamaica, and England, resulting in 37,000 public responses with more than 10,000 baptisms. His sermon books from this period are some of the finest. However, sadly he does not hold to some of the truths today that he preached then.

 **Ruel Lemmons** (1912-1989) became the editor of the *Firm Foundation* in 1955 after the death of G.H.P. Showalter. He remained the editor of the paper until the Showalter family sold the Foundation in 1983 to H. A. "Buster" Dobbs and Bill Cline.

He also edited *Action*, and for five years he edited *Image*. Lemmons preached on every continent and in seventy-nine countries; he was broadcast weekly for eight years over a powerful African radio station that reached an estimated 1,800,000 listeners.

He helped establish Southwestern Christian College in Terrell in 1948. His missionary interest prompted him to establish in 1962 the Pan American Lectures, which he directed for twenty years to encourage missions in Latin America. In 1976 he started a similar lectureship in Europe.

 **Earl Irvin West** (1920-2011) is perhaps the finest student and writer of Restoration History ever to live. He began preaching in Indianapolis as a young man, and preached in different locations over the years. His main work was with the Irvington and Franklin Road congregations in Indianapolis for over 40 years.

He produced five volumes in a series entitled, *Search for the Ancient Order*, the last of which was called *The Trials of the Ancient Order*. Additionally, he wrote biographies on the lives of the gospel preachers, David Lipsomb, Benjamin Franklin, and Hugo McCord.

He wrote extensively for the *Gospel Advocate* and other church related journals for a number of years. He was in high demand for his scholarly research and explanation. He spoke on lectureships around the country.

He spent a number of years at Harding University in Searcy, Arkansas, and at the Harding Graduate School, now Harding School of Theology in Memphis, Tennessee. Many preachers sat at the feet of the great historian and Bible scholar. (cited from theresotrationmovement.com)

E. Claude Gardner (1925) followed H.A. Dixon as president of Freed-Hardeman College in 1969. He retired from FHU in 1990. Through the years he has preached in 365 gospel meetings. He has also written approximately 400 articles for brotherhood publications and a number of books.

Joining brother Gardner on the faculty at Freed-Hardeman were **Tom Holland** and **William Woodson**. While they were prominent preachers during this era, their influence became greater in the years to come.

George W. Bailey was also one of the truly great preachers of this period. His book of sermons in the "Great Preachers of Today" series is in the opinion of many the best of that series and perhaps the best from this period.

Two sons of Gus Nichols – **Flavil** and **Hardeman** – also became great preachers during this period and were influential for years to come. Flavil Nichols preached for approximately 80 years! Hardeman has preached for almost 70 years! Gus Nichols had two more sons who also preached the gospel – **Hudson** and **Foy**. Of his four daughters, three of them married preachers and the fourth was the wife of a faithful deacon. Heaven only knows the good that has been done by this family of faithful servants.

Perry B. Cotham (1912-2013) was another great preacher and debater from this period and for

167

years to come. Brother Cotham began preaching in 1929, and preached for the next 80+ years!

In 1971, brother Cotham left located evangelistic work to become a fulltime traveling evangelist. This work took him into all of the fifty states of America and into all the inhabited continents of the world (over sixty nations). During this time brother Cotham wrote and distributed fourteen different tracts, which were also translated and printed in a number of different languages.

Only heaven knows the depth of brother Perry's contribution to the brotherhood throughout the world. An estimated 15,000 souls were brought to Christ resulting from his missionary efforts in India alone.

New Colleges Established

The **Alabama Christian School of Religion** began in 1967 in Montgomery, AL when in 1966 the governing board of Alabama Christian College voted to discontinue the upper-level program in religious studies in order that the college might seek accreditation as a junior college. **Rex Turner Sr.**, who had served as co-president and then president of Alabama Christian College from its beginning, continued to serve both institutions, Alabama Christian College and Alabama Christian School of Religion, as president until 1973—a total of thirty-one years. At that time, Dr. Turner began to devote his full energies to administration and teaching in the Alabama Christian School of Religion—now *Amridge University.*

Southeastern Institute of the Bible began in 1968 in Florence, AL. Malcolm Hill was asked to come to Florence from Atlanta to begin a Bible college. People in Florence had desired such a school since T.B. Larimore closed Mars Hill in 1887 to devote his time to full-time evangelism. In the late 1920's, a group had tried to bring Freed-Hardeman to Florence. Now, this dream was going to be realized. Malcolm Hill was the school's first president and was followed by **Charles Coil**. The school's name was changed to International Bible College in1971. Dennis Jones became the school's third president in 1989. IBC changed its name to Heritage Christian University when it added its graduate program in 2000.

Malcolm Hill left Florence after five years and returned near his hometown of Livingston, TN, to work with the Sycamore congregation in Cookeville, TN. He would go on to establish **Tennessee Bible College** in 1975. TBC has the distinction of being the first college associated with the churches of Christ to offer the doctor of philosophy degree. This degree is now called the doctor of theology, but the curriculum is the same.

Malcolm Hill served as the school's only president until recently when his son David was named to that position in May of 2010.

Magnolia Bible College began in the fall of 1976 with nine students. The school's home was Kosciusko, Mississippi. Rod Tate was the first President, and Bill Lambert served as Interim President in 1979. **Cecil May, Jr.** became the second president of Magnolia Bible College in 1980. After his retirement in 1997, Gary Kirkendall became Magnolia Bible College's third president and continued in that capacity until the summer of 2000. In November 2000, the board of trustees selected Leslie E. Ferguson, Sr. as the college's fourth president. Dr. Garvis Semore was appointed as the fifth president of Magnolia Bible College in June, 2005. In the fall of 2009 a decision was made to close this school.

The Christian Church Separates from the Disciples of Christ

The Independent Christian Churches/Churches of Christ and the Christian Church (Disciples of Christ) became two distinct bodies over the course of several decades. Troubles stimulated from the Disciples' desire for open membership with the denominations and their desire to join other protestant churches in the first North American Christian Convention (NACC) of 1927.

As a result, a decision was made to organize as into a formal denomination with headquarters and a president, etc. In 1944 at the International Convention of Disciples a "president" was elected who was a proponent of open membership. In 1968, in the Disciples Year Book, Independent churches were removed. Finally in 1971 the Independent churches were listed separately in the Yearbook of American Churches.

AD 70 Controversy

The AD 70 doctrine began troubling the Lord's church when Max King, an elder in the church from Warren, Ohio became the chief proponent back in the early 1970s. He expounded his views through preaching, debating, and in written form. He debated Gus Nichols on his views July 17-20, 1973.

The essence of this theory teaches that when the destruction of Jerusalem took place in September of AD 70, all Bible prophecy was fulfilled: including the second coming of Christ, the resurrection, the final judgment, and the end of the world (or age). Hence the title "Realized Eschatology" is often given to this theory. Overall it means: The study of already-fulfilled last things. Therefore, everything that we generally consider to be still future, according to this doctrine, has already occurred.

A handful of loyal adherents to this doctrine continue debating and preaching to anyone they can get to listen. Overall, however, this movement has had minimal effect in the churches of Christ.

170

The Warren – Flew Debate

On the evenings of September 20-23, 1976 a debate was held in the Coliseum on the campus of North Texas State University in Denton, Texas between Dr. Antony G.N. Flew, Professor of Philosophy at England's Reading University – a world-renowned atheist – and Thomas B. Warren, Professor of Religion and Apologetics at the Harding Graduate School of Religion in Memphis, Tennessee.

Flew abandoned his proposition during the course of the debate admittedly taking more of an agnostic position than that of a positive atheist. Warren, on the other hand, never let up on pressing his points and pressing Flew to answer his arguments. This distinction was the deciding difference in the debate.

Antony Flew was a champion debater, author, teacher and staunch advocate for the atheistic cause. He made headlines, however, in the winter of 2004 by his defection from atheism to deism. Although he did not accept the one true God, he has gone on record to say that biologists' investigation of DNA "has shown, by the almost unbelievable complexity of the arrangements which are needed to produce (life), that intelligence must have been involved..."

The two never debated again. Flew eventually surrendered his position before his death and Warren passed on to his reward. This was indeed a decisive victory for truth. The Warren –Flew Debate proved that for one to know there is no God one would have to be God. To know there is nothing beyond the reaches of this life one must live beyond the reaches of this life. Warren showed us that atheism is an un-provable and therefore untenable, un-defendable doctrine.

Timeline of Events 1961-1980

➢ **1962** – Sunset Bible Institute begins in Lubbock, Texas.

➢ **October 7-14, 1962** – Willard Collins conducts an area-wide meeting in the newly built Nashville Municipal Auditorium.

➢ **August 1964** – Jimmy Allen conducts an area-wide meeting in Dallas which averaged 8,500 in attendance each night. He would conduct another successful meeting in this city in 1966.

➢ **1965** – G.K. Wallace debates Jessie Pratt, overseer of the Church of God of the Union Assembly. Also that year he met James P. Miller in a debate.

➢ **1965** – V.P. Black preaches in a campaign in Mobile, AL, where he lives. 269 souls respond during the meeting. Ninety-eight are baptisms. The same year he preaches in a campaign in Summerville, Georgia, with 191 responses.

➢ **September 1965** – Brown Trail and Bear Valley schools of preaching open.

➢ **February 1966** – The Nashville School of Preaching opens.

➢ **1966** – The Memphis School of Preaching opens.

➢ **1966** – V.P. Black preaches in a campaign in Anniston, Alabama, with 198 responses.

➢ **1967** – The Alabama Christian School of Religion is opened at the building of the College church of Christ in Montgomery.

➢ **1968** – Malcolm Hill becomes the first president of Southeastern Institute of the Bible. Its name was changed to International Bible College in 1971.

➢ **1969** – E. Claude Gardner becomes president of Freed-Hardeman after the death of H.A. Dixon.

172

- ➤ **1969** – The Florida School of Preaching opens.

- ➤ **1971** – The Independent Christian Church is officially recognized as a separate group from the Disciples of Christ.

- ➤ **1971** – The East Tennessee School of Preaching opens.

- ➤ **1975** – Tennessee Bible College begins.

- ➤ **1976** – Magnolia Bible College begins.

- ➤ **September 20-23, 1976** – Thomas B. Warren debates Antony Flew.

- ➤ **September 1, 1977** – Willard Collins becomes present of David Lipscomb University.

- ➤ **1978** – Tennessee Bible College offers first Ph.D. by a church of Christ affiliated school.

- ➤ **1978** – The Southwest School of Preaching opens.

- ➤ **1980** – A written debate is published between Roy C. Deaver and James D. Bales on the subject of marriage, divorce, and remarriage.

Chapter Twelve

The Effects of Change

1981-Present Day

The period under consideration for this chapter is the only period wherein the church has not grown numerically in America. However, the church has grown at an amazing rate on other continents – particularly in Africa, Asia, India, and South America.

In America, the period from 1980 to 1990 saw increase at a rate of 3% in membership and congregations established, while the nation grew by 11%. In 1980 there was an estimation of 1,240,820 members in 12,762 congregations. By 1990 there was an estimation of 1,284,056 members in 13,174 congregations. An estimated 43,236 souls were added to the church during this ten year period as 412 congregations were established.

Growth not only declined but stopped in the years of 1990-2003. In 1990 the church had 1,284,056 members in 13,174 congregations. By 2003 the church had 1,276,533 members in 13,198 congregations. Total membership decreased by 7,523, and only 24 congregations were established.

Today it is estimated that we have 1,178,381 members in 12,240 congregations. Since 1980, the churches of Christ in America have lost an estimated 62,439 members and 522 churches.

The Boston Movement

The Boston Movement or Crossroads Movement caused a lot of damage from the 1970-90's. This movement began in 1967 when **Chuck Lucas** (a minister of the 14th Street congregation in Gainesville, FL) began a program of evangelism for the campus of the University of Florida. Certainly there is nothing wrong with teaching on a college campus, but Lucas had a strange, even cultish way of teaching. He initiated what he called "soul talks" and "prayer partners."

"Soul talks" were prayers and testimonies overseen by a leader who delegated authority over group members. The most intimate details of a person's life were discussed, leading to a cult-like control being exerted by the group leader. "Prayer partners" was a practice of pairing a new Christian with an older "guide." Again the leader would exert a dominant control over the new convert.

In 1972, a young freshman at the University of Florida named **Thomas 'Kip' McKean** was recruited. Over the next several years he would make a name for himself while serving as a "campus minister" for various congregations. While serving for the Heritage church of Christ near Eastern Illinois University in Charleston, Illinois, he was reported in the local press for "tactics of manipulation and control." By the mid-1970's, more than thirty of Lucas' converts fanned out across the country and attached themselves to existing churches of Christ, usually near college campuses. Lucas' discipleship method is now called the "Crossroads Movement." Wherever they went division resulted. At least 200 churches split where campus ministers tried to take over.

In 1979 McKean was offered the position of pulpit and campus minister at the Lexington congregation in Boston. The church was soon renamed the "Boston Church of Christ" and experienced a rapid growth. The Boston Church would plant other churches in Chicago (1982), London (1982), New York City (1983), Providence and Toronto (1985), Johanesberg, Paris, and Stockholm (1986). Also during this time the Boston Church would take over congregations in cities like Atlanta, Indianapolis, and San Francisco, while continuing to establish new ones. By this time it was clear that these "churches" were not churches of Christ.

In August 2, 1987, the *Boston Bulletin* carried an article titled, "The Role of the Evangelist," written by J.P. Tynes. Tynes described the evangelist as being the anointed of God and that to disobey him is the same as disobeying God. These articles were commended by Kip McKean. Later that month another article appeared titled, "Boston – Foreign Pillar Plantings" written by Kip McKean. He divided the world into different areas, with each area having a "pillar" church. This article clearly showed that the Boston Church of Christ is the "mother" church and has the territory of the world.

In the Mid 1980's the practice of rebaptism began. They taught baptism was not valid unless you were one of their disciples first. In 1988 the Crossroads Church disassociated from the Boston Church. On June 26, 1988, McKean wrote that he would become a "Mission Evangelist" and that he would function in the role of the Apostle Paul. From 1986-1989 these colleges banned the Boston Movement from campus: Boston University, Northeastern, Harvard, Tufts, University of Massachusetts, and University of Lowell.

In 1990, McKean left Boston to become the lead evangelist in Los Angeles. In October of 1990, Chris McGrath gave a sermon in Indianapolis in which the singles were limited to dating only on Saturday night from 6 to midnight. In 1993 the Boston Church of Christ officially became the International Church of Christ. In the ICC McKean and his wife Elena were considered the highest authority within the hierarchy of the movement. In February of 1994 the Indianapolis Church of Christ came out publicly against many Boston Church policies. That church loses its "charter" and a loyal Boston "remnant" starts a new church in Indianapolis.

In early 2001, some of the World Sector Leaders (regional evangelists directing geographic areas of churches) began to question the effectiveness of the present leadership structure as well as the qualifications of Kip and Elena McKean to continue in their global leadership role. By September, the issue had reached a head in which the majority of World Sector Leaders agreed that significant changes were necessary. In November 2001, the McKeans announced that they were stepping down from leading the Los Angeles Church of Christ in order to take a sabbatical for an unspecified amount of time in order to focus on "marriage and family issues". All of the McKeans' adult children had disassociated themselves from the movement and though this was not the only issue for the sabbatical, it was a visible 'thorn' in Kip McKean's side.

In 1998, McKean's daughter publicly stated, "I thought that the only place I could find true freedom would be outside the church, and that's the only place that I could be happy." Later, when rumors spread of her actual departure from the ICC, the ICC may have had a consistency issue on its hands: other ICC leaders had been forced to step down after similar occurrences, but what of McKean?

In November 2002, the McKeans announced their resignations from their roles as World Mission Evangelist, Women's Ministry Leader, and Leader of the World Sector Leaders. The World Sector Leaders also announced the disintegration of their leadership group with the suggestion that a new representative leadership group including evangelists, elders and teachers, be formed with an initial meeting in May 2003.

McKean himself attributes the resignation to his daughter's decision to leave the ICC. Later in 2002 the remaining central leadership was officially dissolved at the 2002 'Los Angeles Unity Meeting.' The International Church of Christ administration went under the leadership of Andy Fleming. By the end of 2002, Fleming resigned as the Chairman of the Board.

According to the 2004 International Leadership Conference of affiliated churches, the ICC no longer exists as an organization with a headquarters, structure, or hierarchy where a single church is set up over any other churches; it exists today in a diverse and decentralized state. Some churches have drastically changed their practices (and, in some cases, their names); others carry on in the traditional ICC fashion of assertive evangelism and rebaptism.

In 2003, Kip McKean was invited to return to Oregon's failing Portland International Church of Christ, no longer affiliated with the ICC; he preached his first sermon on July 23. McKean dispatched an anonymous email in October 2006 to Angelino ICC members, deceptively inviting them to a 'bible talk' session where he attempted to recruit them to the Portland Movement. This came to the attention of ICC leaders who responded with a letter advising members to avoid contact with McKean's new organization.

Four months later, McKean led a 'mission team' of 42 Portland-area parishioners to Los Angeles where they joined with 28 local supporters who had begun a new LA church seven months prior. The new group is now called the City of Angels International Christian Church. The movement continues to focus heavily on recruiting from area campuses.

Despite recent loses, the ICC still boasts nearly 100,000 members in 160 nations around the world. However, it has been banned by 39 college campuses and the country of France.

Trickle Down Apostasy and Academics

During this period a greater stress than ever before was placed on academics in the colleges which operated Bible Departments. To understand what has happened and is happening in these schools one must understand the direction they decided to go. In the mid-twentieth century many of our schools began seeking regional accreditation in order to advance to four-year colleges and later universities. Being accredited gave many Christians the opportunity to learn at a Christian school and be universally recognized as qualified for various professions such as school teachers and businessmen. Certainly nothing is wrong with these desires and many faithful Christians understood the value of accreditation.

However, accreditation also meant that worldly committees, which knew nothing about sound doctrine and Bible teaching, would have the first and final say on who was qualified to teach Bible in our affiliated universities. The accrediting bodies required that the schools choose their faculties based upon the advanced degrees they held, rather than faithfulness to the word. Schools began to covet the men who had earned doctorates in order to appease accrediting associations. Our men who wanted to teach had to go into state schools or denominational seminaries to become qualified. We acknowledge that it is possible for a man of great maturity to go through the years of graduate study in a theological seminary without being damaged; but it is very exceptional.

The falsehoods learned in such places were brought back into our colleges and universities and "trickled down" to the preacher students. The preacher students then promoted these doctrines in the church. Herein is the root of the "Change Agent" movement and the new hermeneutic being taught by many today.

Some of the colleges still have some very good men in their Bible Departments. However, a good number of the schools have been given wholly to the change agent movement which erupted during this period. The textbooks now used and the outside reading they recommend to their students are overwhelmingly books written by men and women who are not members of the church. One needs only to look at the books on the recommended lists at a Christian university to see how far they have drifted.

A second problem which resulted from this decision to become accredited is that practical ministry and evangelism is not now as important as scholarship. A greater emphasis is given to term papers and book reviews, citing and pertaining to the works of denominational "scholars" than is given to proper interpretation and presentation of the truth. Moreover, the rigors of academic study often tend to develop a trend which is unprofitable for ministry. Preachers tend to be more comfortable in their library studying than conducting Bible studies with lost souls. Also, the preacher tends to preach more like he is lecturing in a college classroom than exhorting sinners to repent. Students do tend to pick up on the tendencies of their teachers. When the teachers are strictly academically minded men, the students will be more likely to be strictly academic. When the teachers are soul-winners and faithful gospel preachers, the students are more likely to become soul-winners and faithful preachers.

The only hope for the future of Bible teaching in the Christian universities is for these schools to assert their right to re-take control of their Bible departments, even though this action may risk the displeasure of the accrediting associations.

The Influence of Liberalism/Change Agents

The influence of Garrett and Ketcherside during this period can be eerily compared to J.H. Garrison and the liberal movement that wrecked the church in the 19th Century. The change agents are arguing for a "new hermeneutic" for interpreting scripture. Rather than seeking examples, and statements or commands from the Bible as a means of guidance, they view the Bible strictly as a narrative or story. Inspiration is questioned, if not completely denied. Stress is placed upon a "grace only" system of salvation instead of recognizing God's commands and the authority of His word.

Some points of controversy include:

- A type of **neo-Pentecostalism** became apparent in some congregations. It has been claimed by change agents that the Holy

Spirit is guiding them through direct and personal revelation. In the 1970's **Pat Boone** became an example of someone who claimed to have the gift of speaking in tongues, etc. In 1988 **Don Finto** of the Belmont congregation in Nashville claimed to be an apostle with worldwide authority.

- **Unity with denominations** is argued. To argue this point, the church must be viewed as a denomination resulting from the Restoration Movement. However, as we have learned, the men who advocated restoration never sought to establish another denomination, but to return to the faith and practice of the New Testament church. In the 1980's **Rubel Shelly** of Nashville began urging unity with protestant denominations, much as did the Disciples in the early 20th Century. **Rick Atchley**, **Mike Cope**, **Randy Harris**, **Lynn Anderson**, **Douglas Foster**, and **Jeff Walling** would also have to be included in this movement.

- **Re-Baptism** once again became a topic of debate. It was argued that denominational baptisms could be accepted by churches, and that one did not have to be baptized for the remission of sins.

- In the 1990's **Max Lucado** began preaching the sinner's prayer rather than baptism for the remission of sins (Acts 2:38).

- As in the 19th a few churches have begun to use **instrumental music** in worship.

- A **missionary society approach** to benevolent work and mission work is again persistent, as agencies and organizations under various boards of directors are attempting to do the work of the church in the place of the church.

- The **role of women in the church** has been expanded to include the deaconess and other ministerial roles. (See 1 Timothy 3:8 ff. for the qualifications of a deacon.)

- **Grace** has been misconstrued to follow the teachings of Augustine and Calvin rather than the teachings of Christ. Change agents teach that grace and law are mutually exclusive.

- Many of these congregations are also removing the name "Church of Christ" from their signs and buildings. They are becoming **"community churches"** instead.

- **Moral issues** such as immodest dress, social drinking, marriage, divorce, and remarriage were scoffed at and redefined.

- Literal **translations of the Bible** have been replaced by dynamic equivalencies and modern perversions of scripture.

- In 2003, **F. LaGard Smith** wrote a book titled "After Life" in which he denied the eternality of hell as a place of ongoing conscious torment for the wicked.

- **John Mark Hicks'** book *Come to the Table* suggests that we should change the way we partake of the Lord's Supper. He also helped to begin a congregation in Nashville in which mechanical instruments are used in worship, and women have a leading role in the worship.

- Change agents have sought to promote their views on such programs as the **Tulsa Soul-Winning Workshop**; the now defunct **Nashville Jubilee**; college lectureships such as **Abilene, Lipscomb, Harding Graduate School**, and **Pepperdine**; and the **Scholars' Conference**. **Winterfest** has also become an activity for youth programs in liberal churches.

Many of these men have begun writing their own revisionist view of restoration history. You will remember that this was also one of the agendas of the progressive movement in the 19th Century. Another agenda of this movement in recent years is to align themselves with the Independent Christian Church.

Wineskins magazine became the prominent publication of this group. Also, the **Christian Chronicle** (published by Oklahoma Christian University) has become sympathetic with this movement and advertises its events. **Restoration Quarterly** should also be included in the list of papers which helped to advocate liberalism in the church during this time.

Standing in the Gap

While this has been a turbulent time in the church and in society in general, let us not lose sight of the many great works and great preachers who have "done all to stand." Gospel meetings began to be shortened in the second half of the twentieth century to Sunday-Wednesday events. In addition to preachers mentioned in the years prior, we should also note others who held many gospel meetings during this period.

Maxie Boren and **Gary Colley, Sr.** have each held approximately 700 gospel meetings in their lives respectively. **Robert R. Taylor, Jr., Garland Elkins, James Meadows,** and **Tom Holland** may have eclipsed that number. Others who held hundreds of meetings during this period include **Wendell Winkler, Bobby Duncan, Charles Coil, Johnny Ramsey**, and **Andrew Connally**.

Freed-Hardeman University continued to wield a tremendous influence with conservative churches during this period. Many of the men who taught there during this period have also held hundreds of gospel meetings.

Wayne Jackson has opposed the change agents through his paper the *Christian Courier*. **Dave Miller, Frank Chesser, Curtis Cates, Wayne Coats,** and **Gobel Music** and many others have written books to address change agents and their doctrines as well.

Garland Robinson began *Seek the Old Paths* as a means of warning brethren against the rise of liberalism in the church. **Buster Dobbs** bought the *Firm Foundation* and used his editorials to speak against the liberalism in the colleges – particularly Abilene Christian University.

Alan Highers became the editor of the *Spiritual Sword* and continued to use the paper to warn brethren against the liberal agenda. **Jim Laws** was the associate editor.

Garland Elkins began a new journal at the Southaven, Mississippi congregation – *Power*. The congregation also went on to host the Power Lectures.

Bill Dillon began a paper titled the *Gospel Gleaner*. While the primary emphasis of the *Gleaner* was evangelism, the paper was never afraid to address controversial issues. **Max R. Miller** was also a guiding influence in the paper, and *First Century Christian*. **J.C. Choate**, a missionary, began *Voice of Truth International*. **Basil Overton** began the *World Evangelist*.

Apologetics Press was a new venture in religious journalism among churches of Christ. This publishing company focuses primarily upon Christian evidences and higher criticism of the Bible in defense of those who would attack the Scriptures. Their primary paper is *Reason and Revelation*.

Much like the period of the 1850s-1900, three groups existed in the church. One group stood to the left and conducted a campaign to bring liberalism into the church. One group stood to the right and opposed them at every turn. The third group stood in between these two – accepting some of the ideas presented by the change agents while rejecting some. **Furman Kearley** was more of an academically minded man and edited the Gospel Advocate for much of this period. The *Advocate* was criticized by many for not making a stand against many of the issues being introduced into the church during this period. **Jim Bill McInteer** took a similar position with the *20th Century Christian*. Many of the colleges and their presidents have also attempted to take this "middle of the road" stand during this period.

Television, Radio, and Internet

Mack Lyon was the voice of *In Search of the Lord's Way*, has introduced millions of viewers to the plea of restoring New Testament Christianity. **James Watkins** also had a very popular program titled, *Preaching the Gospel*.

Winfred Claiborne was known nationally as the voice of the International Gospel Hour.

In November of 2005, the Highland congregation in Dalton, Georgia, began the **Gospel Broadcasting Network** which broadcasts New Testament Christianity 24/7. The church in Southaven, Mississippi now oversees the work.

Many congregations are using local cable companies to broadcast their own television Bible studies. Many churches and preachers are also making good use of the internet. Much of the information being circulated today is being circulated via the internet. Many colleges are also using the internet to broaden their distance learning programs.

Schools of Preaching Continue and Flourish

As more and more colleges began to introduce false teachings through their Bible Departments, congregations began to take back the responsibility to train preachers. This period has seen a few more schools of preaching added to the landscape. However, a few have adopted a different format, using night classes.

Jim McGill was a visionary in this regard. Brother McGill was Director of the Nashville School of Preaching when he implemented a more student friendly curriculum. The school grew from around 30 students to over 220 students under his direction. In 2002, he helped establish the Middle Tennessee School of Preaching. He also helped the Georgia School of Preaching to be formatted in this way. **Jim Lewis**, one of McGill's teachers at Nashville, began a similar program with the Chattanooga School of Preaching in January of 2000.

Wesley Simons, one of McGill's students at Tennessee Bible College and graduate of the Memphis School of Preaching, helped begin a fulltime program the Tri-Cities School of Preaching in August, 2001.

The West Virginia School of Preaching opened in August of 1994 with faculty of Wirt Cook, Denver Cooper, Emanuel Daugherty, Charles Pugh III, W. Terry Varner, D. Gene West, Bert Jones, and Steve Stevens.

The Northwest Florida School of Preaching and its predecessor, the Bellview School of Preaching, have operated in the Pensacola area. The Milestone congregation now oversees this work.

In 2003, former missionary to Zambia, Jerry Sullins, became the first director of the Bible Institute of Missouri, a preaching school operated by the Kansas Expressway church of Christ in Springfield, Missouri.

Lectureships

During this period when college lectureships began to promote liberalism, churches began conducting lectureships of their own. Countless congregations across the country have hosted annual lectureships for decades now. Many of them also publish lectureship books to go along with their program.

Perhaps the most popular lectureship to date, in addition to the annual Bible Lectureship at Freed-Hardeman University, is **Polishing the Pulpit**. It is overseen by the Jacksonville, Alabama congregation and is conducted annually in Sevierville, Tennessee. The lectureship features many excellent speakers and is a great source of encouragement to those who attend. It has been questioned, however, for its practice of charging admission to attend the event.

Timeline of Events 1981- Present Day

➢ **1980-82** – The Boston Movement becomes an entity which officially became the International Church of Christ in 1993.

➢ **March, 1983** – In Centerville, Tennessee, at a preachers' forum, Rubel Shelly apologizes for having preached that there is one church, deeming such a message to be sectarian.

➢ **1984** – The Collinsville, Oklahoma church of Christ was sued by a former member after they publicly withdrew fellowship from her. Garland Elkins, along with a small group of Christians, appeared on the Phil Donahue Show, a nationally syndicated television show, to defend the church's right to withdraw fellowship in keeping with the Scriptures.

➢ **1988** – Don Finto of Nashville, Tennessee claims to have been called to be an apostle with worldwide authority.

➢ **1990s** – The Nashville Jubilee is conducted over a period of several years to promote liberalism in the church. The event closes due to underwhelming support.

➢ **1994** – The Jacksonville, Alabama church of Christ begins a program for preachers titled, "Polishing the Pulpit." The program has become one of the largest gatherings among churches with more than 4,000 attendees meeting annually in Sevierville, Tennessee.

➢ **October, 1998** – Wayne Jackson begins publishing an online edition of the *Christian Courier*. It has become one of the most widely used websites among church members.

➢ **February, 2000** – Challenge Youth Conference (CYC) begins and eventually draws thousands annually in different locations.

- ➢ **2000's** – Although it began in 1968, by the 2000's Lads to Leaders became the largest single program for training young people among churches of Christ, drawing tens of thousands to its different locations each year.

- ➢ **November, 2005** – The Highland church of Christ in Dalton, Georgia begins the Gospel Broadcasting Network. The work is now overseen by the Southaven, Mississippi congregation.

- ➢ **June, 2008** – The *Firm Foundation* ceases publication after 124 years. It has recently been restarted in electronic format.

- ➢ **2009 – Churches of Christ in America number an estimated 1,224,404 members in 12,629 congregations.**

- ➢ **December, 2009** – Magnolia Bible College closes.

- ➢ **May, 2011** – Michael Shank publishes his conversion account in the book *Muscle and a Shovel*. The book became a best-seller among churches of Christ, and has been instrumental in over 50,000 people obeying the gospel..

- ➢ **2015 – Churches of Christ in America number an estimated 1,178,381 members in 12,240 congregations**

- ➢ **2017** – The Tulsa Workshop, known for its left-wing agenda, ceases meeting due to dwindling numbers.

Chapter Thirteen

Where Do We Go from Here?

"Who is left among you who saw this temple in its former glory? And how do you see it now? In comparison with it, is this not in your eyes as nothing?" (Haggai 2:3)

Oftentimes such studies as this will leave us considering the temple (the church) in its former glory, while the church of today is as nothing in our eyes. But just as the glory of the latter temple (ultimately the church) would exceed the glory of Solomon's temple (Haggai 2:9), so too can the glory of the church of tomorrow exceed the glory of the church of yesterday.

We have advantages never before known to Christians. Technology has made communication much easier than ever before. We are blessed with money in abundance. We have facilities, transportation, manpower, talent, education, and opportunity like never before. Most of all, we have the Lord. We are His servants. His promises remain. "If God is for us, who can be against us?" (Romans 8:31)

We must believe that the best years are ahead. The world is a big place and billions of people still need the gospel. Not only must we believe that the best years are ahead, we must work to see that this is true.

A Need for Revival

Before we can seize the opportunities set before us, we must have a revival. Our hearts must be humbled to repentance and our spirits must be stirred to action. As always, we must have the attitude that "revival begins with me." Revival must begin within the local congregation as well.

A great many lessons can be learned from Jesus' words to the seven churches of Asia (Revelation 2-3). Jesus was concerned with two ideas in His letters to these churches. He was concerned with (1) their works; and (2) their faithfulness. He said nothing of numbers, buildings, colleges, papers, etc. When the church at Ephesus had left their first love, they were told (1) to remember from whence they had fallen, (2) to repent, and (3) to do the first works. *Remember*, *repent*, and *return*. We must do the same to-day.

Jesus addressed seven *churches*. He did not address seven colleges, missionary societies, lectureship committees, or editors. Christ's concern has always been with the church. Until we make the local church our primary concern again, we will not repeat the success of the past generations who did. Our first love should be for the Lord, His word, and His church. Many of us have left this "first love." We must *remember* what it was like when the church was our first love, *repent*, and *return*.

Each congregation must place an emphasis on the spiritual growth and maturity of that church. If every local congregation will determine to be faithful, the overall body will be more faithful. Each congregation must also place an emphasis on filling their communities with the doctrine of Christ (Acts 5:28). If each congregation will do their very best to evangelize in their hometown, the church as a whole will grow. Seeing that the church has lost an estimated 62,439 members and 522 churches since 1980, we must realize the need to be more evangelistic.

Moreover, great churches are comprised of great families. We must do a better job of keeping our children in the church. We must teach them to distinguish biblical Christianity from denominationalism. We must teach them to marry faithful Christians and to raise faithful Christians. If we will do a better job of keeping our children in the church, many churches will have to tear down their buildings and build greater ones, instead of closing.

We must also remain separate from the world. The issue of marriage, divorce, and remarriage which constitutes adultery is not going away (Matthew 19:9-10). Many of the moral issues confronting the church are not going away, but only growing worse.

Worldliness in the church is killing the church. We cannot let up on Jesus' plan for the church to be a light in the world of darkness and a city set on a hill. Let us remember that we represent Him and call each other back to biblical morality. "Love not the world..." (1 John 2:15-17). Love the Lord. Love the truth. Love each other! But let us realize that a little of the world's leaven will leaven the whole lump (1 Corinthians 5:6 ff).

"Be Thou Faithful"

Our study has also observed a number of remarkable occurrences over the past 200 years concerning biblically conservative and biblically liberal ideologies. Just as the Disciples of Christ and the International Church of Christ have lost members and momentum after severing from the body of Christ at large, so too has the recent liberal movement in the church. The only foothold they have among us is within our universities. And as long as we mandate that the Bible departments of these schools comply with regional accreditation, the liberals will continue to have a voice in these schools.

Yet, we have also seen events like the Jubilee in Nashville and the Tulsa Workshop ending with a thud. The youth gathering "Winterfest" which is controlled by the liberal element in the church has also diminished in recent years. Whereas events like Polishing the Pulpit, Challenge Youth Conference, and Lads to Leaders are growing every year. While left-wing television programs like the "Herald of Truth" are barely mentioned or considered anymore, conservative brethren have established an entire television broadcasting network – the Gospel Broadcasting Network.

Moreover, while some of the larger liberal churches have plateaued and many are now losing numbers. Such losses are inevitable when more time is spent being ecumenical, rather than being evangelistic. These churches now have women preachers, contemporary worship, and all sorts of denominational practices, attempting to woo the denominational world into fellowship with them. However, the hope of restoring New Testament Christianity is no longer important to them. They have become just another denomination in the eyes of the world and one another.

Let their demise serve as a warning to everyone. Let us not be as treacherous Judah, who did not learn from her backsliding sister, Israel (Jeremiah 3:7-8). Rather, let us seek the old paths and walk therein (Jeremiah 6:16). Each congregation must strive toward the greater good of serving the Lord faithfully in all things.

From the Eden of Genesis to the Eden of Revelation, obedience to God is a silver thread which runs throughout the Bible. God requires our obedience. It is the "whole of man" (Ecclesiastes 12:13). When man disobeyed God, he was expelled from the Eden of Genesis; and only those who repent and obey God will be allowed to enter the Eden of Revelation (Revelation 22:14). When a church disobeys God and begins compromising with the world, it ceases to be the Lord's church and becomes the world's church. Such congregations must repent if they hope to have any future blessed by God. We plead with these brethren to *remember, repent,* and *return.*

Conclusion

The Bible and history have taught us that if we will remain faithful, God will provide the increase (1 Corinthians 3:6 ff.). Let us work while it is day, practice goodwill toward every man while we have opportunity, and sow and water the seed of the kingdom wherever we can.

If we will be faithful to God, God will be even more faithful to us. Man can never be as faithful to God as God is to man. We simply cannot "out give" God. Let us determine to do all the good we can do; to all the people we can help; in all the places we can minister; for as long as we can serve.

What will history say about this generation? How will we be remembered? If the Lord wills, someone will be writing a history of this generation one hundred years from now. What will they say? Will it be said that this generation overcame worldliness, kept a steadfast spirit, and led future generations in their faithfulness to the Lord? Or, will it be said that this generation gave in to worldliness, was overcome by the world, and continued to lose more members and more congregations? And so we must ask, do we intend to be a blessing or a curse to our children and our children's children?

We are at a crossroads. It is a historic time in the history of the Restoration. The Lord's church is growing wonderfully well overseas, but declining in America. What can we do to build up the church in this country? The answer to our future lies in our past. This is not the first time the church has had to overcome tribulation, and it may not be the last. We must hold fast to the cross, the church, and the word of God. We must put the focus back on faithfulness, obedience, evangelism, and the local church. If we will do these things, there is no reason not to believe that future generations will be blessed by our faithfulness and thankful for our contribution to their history.

Resources

*A special mention must be made of **Scott Harp's** invaluable website **www.therestorationmovement.com** without which much of the material in this book would not appear.*

Baxter, William, *Life of Elder Walter Scott*

Boles, H. Leo, *Biographical Sketches of Gospel Preachers*

Boles, Leo Lipscomb, and J.E. Choate, *I'll Stand on the Rock: Biography of H. Leo Boles*

Borden, Eli Monroe, *Life, Incidents, and Sermons of Eli Monroe Borden*

Campbell, Alexander, *Memoirs of Elder Thomas Campbell*

Campbell, Thomas, *Declaration and Address of the Christian Association of Washington County, PA*

Cato, Willie, *His Hand and Heart: The Wit and Wisdom of Marshall Keeble*

Choate, J.E., *Roll Jordan Roll: A Biography of Marshall Keeble*

Collins, Artie, *Ramblings of an Old Preacher: Memoirs of Artie Collins*

Donan, P., *Jacob Creath, Jr.: Pioneer Preacher*

Doran, Adron, and J.E. Choate, *The Christian Scholar: A Biography of Hall Laurie Calhoun*

Elliott, B. Raymond, *Ann Street Memories: The Early Years of Montgomery Bible School and Alabama Christian College (1940s and 1950s)*

Erwin, Andrew D., *You've Been a Good Brother, Willie: The Life and Sermons of W.A. Bradfield*

Foster, Douglas A., Paul M. Blowers, Anthony L. Dunnavant, and D. Newell Williams (eds.), *The Encyclopedia of the Stone-Campbell Movement*

Franklin, Joseph, and J.A. Headington, *Life of Elder Benjamin Franklin*

Gardner, James, *The Christians of New England*

Goodpasture, B.C., *Marshall Keeble: Biography and Sermons*

Gray, Joe D., *Unity in the Midst of Slavery and War*

Humble, Bill, *The Missionary Society Controversy in the Restoration Movement (1823-1875)*

_____, *The Story of the Restoration*

Jenkins, Ancil, *A.G. Freed: Biography of a Gentleman*

Kilgore, Charles Franklin, *The James O'Kelly Schism in the Methodist Episcopal Church*

Lambert, Gussie, *In Memoriam*

Lewis, Jack P., *As I Remember It: An Autobiography*

Lipscomb, David, *Jesse L. Sewell: Early Tennessee Preacher*

Lockwood, Bill, *Events in the Life of Joe S. Warlick: The Years of His Early Life (1865-1901)*

McClean, Archibald, *Alexander Campbell as a Preacher*

McCoy, V. Glenn, *Return to the Old Paths: A History of the Restoration Movement*

McDade, Gary (ed.), *The Glory of Preaching: The Twenty-Sixth Annual Spiritual Sword Lectureship*

201

McGill, James R., Various articles which have appeared in the *Gospel Gleaner*, *Gospel Preacher*, and *Searching the Scriptures Quarterly*

McMillon, Lynn, *Restoration Roots: The Scottish Origins of the American Restoration Movement*

Morgan, Boyd, *Arkansas Angels*

Morrison, Matthew C., *Like a Lion: Daniel Sommer's Seventy Years of Preaching*

Morro, W.C., *Brother McGarvey: The Life of President J.W. McGarvey of the College of the Bible, Lexington, Kentucky*

Patterson, Noble, and Terry J. Gardner, *Foy E. Wallace, Jr.: Soldier of the Cross*

Phillips, Dabney, *Medley of the Restoration: Inspirational Insights into the Restoration Movement*

_____, *Restoration Principles and Personalities*

Powell, J.M., and Mary Nelle Hardeman Powers, *N.B.H.: A Biography of Nicholas Brodie Hardeman*

_____, *The Man from Mars Hill: The Life and Times of T.B. Larimore*

Robinson, Edward J., *Show Us How You Do It: Marshall Keeble and the Rise of Black Churches of Christ in the United States (1914-1968)*

Richardson, Robert, *Memoirs of Alexander Campbell*

Rogers, W.C., *Recollections of Men of Faith*

Scobey, James E., *Franklin College and Its Influences*

Sears, Lloyd Cline, *The Eyes of Jehovah: The Life and Faith of James Alexander Harding*

Smith, Lloyd L., *Gospel Preachers of Yesteryear*

Smithson, John T. III, *Tracing Our Steps: A Chronology of the Restoration Movement* (vols. 1-2)

Srygley, F.D., *Smiles and Tears or Larimore and His Boys*

Tant, Yater, *J.D. Tant: Texas Preacher*

Taylor, Irene C., *My Heart Standeth in Awe of Thy Word: A Brief Biography of Robert R. Taylor, Jr.*

Underwood, Maude Jones, *C.R. Nichol: A Preacher of Righteousness*

West, Earl, *Elder Ben Franklin: Eye of the Storm*

_____, *The Enchanted Knight: The Life Story of Hugo McCord*

_____, *The Life and Times of David Lipscomb*

_____, *The Search for the Ancient Order* (vols. 1-4)

Wilburn, James R., *The Hazzard of the Die: Tolbert Fanning and the Restoration Movement*

Williams, John Augustus, *Life of Elder "Raccoon" John Smith*

Wilson, Michael, *Arkansas Christians: A History of the Restoration Movement in Randolph County, AR (1800-1995)*